# Bernstein's
# Orchestral Music

*Unlocking the Masters Series, No. 22*

# Bernstein's Orchestral Music

## An Owner's Manual

David Hurwitz

AMADEUS
PRESS

An Imprint of Hal Leonard Corporation
New York

Published in 2011 by Amadeus Press
An Imprint of Hal Leonard Corporation
7777 West Bluemound Road
Milwaukee, WI 53213

Trade Book Division Editorial Offices
33 Plymouth St., Montclair, NJ 07042


Printed in the United States of America


Book design by Snow Creative Services


Library of Congress Cataloging-in-Publication Data

Hurwitz, David, 1961–
    Bernstein's orchestral music : an owner's manual / David Hurwitz.
       p. cm. — (Unlocking the masters series ; no. 22)
    ISBN 978-1-57467-193-3
    1. Bernstein, Leonard, 1918–1990. Orchestra music.  2. Orchestral music—20th century—History and criticism.  I. Title.
    ML410.B566H87 2011
    784.2092—dc22

                                                                    2011000283


www.amadeuspress.com

To my friend and partner in crime, David Vernier.

This was his suggestion.

# Contents

# Preface

This book contains descriptions of all of Leonard Bernstein's orchestral music for the concert hall, some twenty pieces. They range from large-scale symphonies and concertos, to ballets, overtures, and tiny occasional works just a couple of minutes long. Since his death in 1990, other hands have assembled suites of extracts from his theatrical works, specifically *Candide*, *A Quiet Place*, and *1600 Pennsylvania Avenue*, and there's an orchestration of the song cycle *Arias and Barcarolles* as well, but they have not been included as they were not prepared by Bernstein himself (which doesn't meant that they're not well made and worth hearing). There is more than enough *echt-*Bernstein to provide a generous taste of his music from all periods without recourse to posthumous arrangements.

I have also not undertaken to write full discussions of his musical comedies and his single grand opera, *A Quiet Place*. In the case of the former, Bernstein's classic status as a composer was established long ago, and their overtures and concert suites are included here. However, there has always been a distinction made between music written for the stage and that for the concert hall, one which I wish to respect. The reason for this is simple. If you want to be taken seriously as a twentieth-century classical composer and you are not working almost exclusively in the field of opera, then your reputation will rest on your output of concert music. This includes theatrical works such as ballets that can double as freestanding orchestral pieces. The vast majority of Bernstein's music falls into this category.

This fact tells us, more than anything else he may have said, about how he regarded his work as a composer, and how he wanted to be remembered. Leonard Bernstein was seldom at a loss for words, and yet his music speaks to us even more eloquently about his vision and his intentions. Interestingly, if you look at his statements in the prefaces he wrote to his scores (and I quote many of them), he seemed curiously reticent to discuss the music in detail. This doesn't mean that his own comments were not insightful or valuable; but as one of the most knowledgeable and experienced performers of the last century, one who worked daily with the great masterpieces of the classical repertoire, Bernstein understood that ultimately the music must speak for itself and find its way into the world independently of the personality of its creator and first interpreter—however powerful and magnetic that may have been.

This process is ongoing. Some of Bernstein's music has achieved classic status and some of it, particularly his later works, has not. There is no way to tell what the ultimate outcome will be. In this respect, there's a difference between writing a book about long-established masterpieces, and one about newer works still undergoing the "weathering" process that will determine their fate. When talking about repertory standards I can say, "It's all wonderful and valuable even if you don't like it immediately," and be believed, or at least have the weight of history on my side. That isn't the case here. Bernstein's music, not so much because of what it is, but because of our relationship to it as listeners at this particular time, asks us to play an active role in the process by which "music" becomes "classical music." This is an exciting prospect. Your opinion matters.

As with previous books in this series, the discussion below consists of descriptions, and not analyses, of the various works. Their point is to give you a sense of how the music sounds, what characteristics typify Bernstein the composer, and how best to approach each piece as a listener. Also very important, in my view, is the opportunity to survey Bernstein's orchestral output as a whole, over the entire span of his career. Composers in prior centuries had a big advantage over their colleagues today, one that I can sum up in a single word: ignorance. There was no body of "classical music" as we understand it, and there was no prejudice against modern music. Old was bad, new was good, with the proviso that the new had to make some effort to please its audience. Listeners demanded and welcomed novelty, at least up to a point.

This situation began to change in the late nineteenth century. The first composer to really feel the crushing weight of musical history was Brahms, and the situation has only gotten more difficult since then. How does a composer balance often conflicting demands to write music that's progressive but also comprehensible, innovative in style but also traditional as to form and genre, personal in utterance but also able to withstand comparison to hundreds of years of certified classical masterpieces? It's a tall order, though not an impossible one. The number of contemporary composers who walk this particular tightrope successfully will always be small, and our proximity to them in time can make them hard to identify.

My hope is that this book makes the case that Bernstein belongs in this select group. His music deserves to survive for all of the most plausible artistic and musical reasons: shapeliness of form, depth and range of expression, melodic beauty, mastery of orchestral writing, and sincerity of utterance. You may not like all of it equally—I don't. That's normal. Not all of these works may survive the pitiless winnowing process that determines what becomes a "classic." However, what I do believe, and very strongly, is that they are all good music. Bernstein knew what he was doing. His pieces are worth getting to know, and they reward the time you spend making their acquaintance. For now that is all we have the right and reason to expect. Surely, it's enough.

# Acknowledgments

The author wishes to acknowledge with gratitude the assistance of Boosey & Hawkes in sourcing the scores of *Songfest* and *Dybbuk*, and to thank editor extraordinaire Bob Levine for his patience and encouragement.

# Bernstein's
# Orchestral Music

# Introduction

# *A Great Composer?*

In her autobiography *In My Own Voice*, the great mezzo-soprano Christa Ludwig wrote: "There is an enormous difference between a brilliant musician and a genius, and Bernstein was a genius." This is probably the most insightful and intelligent single remark ever made about him, and it explains a great deal about the problems that arise in considering Bernstein's achievement as a composer. His genius was of a particularly omnivorous kind. He was good at everything he did, and he loved doing it all: conducting, teaching, writing, making television programs, and composing. There weren't enough hours in the day, days in the year, or years in a single life, to achieve everything that he knew he could do, and was driven by his genius to attempt. The body also imposes its own physical limits, as his death on October 14, 1990, at the relatively young age of seventy-two clearly showed. Yet it's strangely fitting that five days after announcing his official retirement from conducting, he was gone. The notion of Bernstein suffering enforced inactivity, the result of illness, and waiting passively for death, is unimaginable.

Evaluating Bernstein's compositional legacy presents challenges to scholars and historians because normal people tend to judge others by their own standards and have difficulties coming to grips with the multitasking ability of a genius. The usual story goes something like this: Bernstein was a promising composer who wasted too much of his talent working as a conductor, a mere entertainer, when he should have been writing more masterpieces. This particular line of reasoning got a boost from the great man himself, who liked to complain that he needed to take time off from conducting for composing, and also by the fact that, with a few exceptions, the late works are not as popular and successful as were the pieces that appeared roughly from the 1940s through the early 1960s.

To be sure, Bernstein's career as a composer had its disappointments. His last musical, *1600 Pennsylvania Avenue*, was a flop. His opera *A Quiet Place*, despite its inclusion of the splendid, earlier *Trouble in Tahiti*, which became most of the second act, hasn't caught on and perhaps it never will. But make no mistake: Bernstein was as great a composer as he was a conductor, and it's rather odd to see his stature minimized on the basis of sheer quantity rather than quality. He composed more orchestral music than did, say, Brahms, Ravel, or Debussy. The Deutsche Grammophon edition featuring him conducting his own pieces occupies twelve well-filled compact discs (and it is by no means complete). That's at least as long as your average Mahler or Bruckner symphony cycle.

More to the point, he was a superb craftsman, an inveterate reviser and polisher of his finished works, and a perfectionist with a genius's eye for detail. After all, who knew more than he did about what constitutes a musical masterpiece? If he didn't churn out tons of stuff—not incidentally avoiding the charge that he was facile, formulaic, or shallow by virtue of excessive productivity—then it's the particular standard to which he is being held that needs revising. We also must be careful not to let Bernstein's own frustrations color our view of his achievement. Tchaikovsky, for example, was another composer who had very harsh things to say about many of his greatest and most beloved works. Still, there is a very real sense in which Bernstein the polymath is the enemy of Bernstein the great composer. His personality was so huge, so voracious, and so very public, that it's quite easy to lose the music in considering the man.

To avoid this pitfall, I propose to consider Bernstein the composer one work at a time, describing each piece and evaluating it on its own merits, according to purely musical criteria. I will discuss issues such as form, orchestration, melody, harmony, expressive content—but not biography, and above all none of that "story behind the music" business that invariably shifts the focus away from the work itself, and what it so clearly wants to tell us. Bernstein's so-called "serious" music deserves at least that much consideration, and more important, it certainly withstands this sort of scrutiny. Like the man, these pieces are big, bold, emotionally generous, warmhearted, and richly textured. They are works of genius.

At this point, you may well want to move on to the music, and you should feel free to do so. However, I'd like to take a little more time to discuss why Bernstein's work perhaps has not received the recognition that it deserves from much of the classical music community. The reasons are interesting, and offer a telling commentary on how the performing arts business operates. They also shed valuable light on the kind of composer that Bernstein was, what he was trying to achieve, and the context in which his works might best be viewed, at least as compared with others of their type. From our perspective today, some two decades after his death, we can see very clearly that he was both more forward looking and more central to contemporary aesthetic concerns than he appeared for much of the latter half of the twentieth century.

## The Atonal "Interruption"

At the present time, when contemporary composers are once again embracing tonality and (sometimes) melody, it's difficult to understand the hostility that such composers as Bernstein faced. Had he not been a conductor who was in a position to promote his own music, he might well have been offered far less attention as a creative artist than he received. This is not the place to go into an extensive analysis as to why twentieth-century "art music" embraced an unpopular musical dead end like atonality, but it had a lot to do with the institutionalization of the performing arts as embodied in the subsidized European system, the American equivalent of which is the "not-for-profit" corporation. This freed composers and performers from the irritating necessity of earning a living from paying audiences, and thus from the responsibility of creating music that that those audiences might enjoy listening to.

Of course, most of these people still would not have been able to earn a living through commissions; that has always been the exception, even with more tradition-minded composers who achieved a measure of popularity in their own lifetime. So they did the next worst thing: they taught. Thus ensconced in tenured positions at universities and conservatories, they were able to destroy a couple of generations of budding artists with their doctrinaire nonsense. It's important to stress in this connection that atonal or twelve-tone composition is neither good nor bad in and of itself. Great works have been written using this style, and doubtless will continue to be. The "classical" composers of the Second Viennese School (Schoenberg, Berg, and Webern) were also musicians of tremendous originality and importance whose innovations only became obnoxious when they ceased to be manifestations of their individual genius and became rules to be applied mechanically and thoughtlessly.

Numerous other composers also found distinctive means of employing twelve-tone, atonal, or serial techniques (they don't mean the same thing, but for our purposes can be used interchangeably) to create a significant and perhaps enduring body of work. Four names that spring immediately to mind in this connection are Igor Stravinsky, Frank Martin, Roger Sessions, and Einojuhani Rautavaara (the latter still going strong at the time of writing). Even Bernstein explored the technique successfully as part of his famously inclusive eclecticism. We will see where in due course. But the fact remains that composers who did not toe the party line in the 1960s and '70s were treated with scorn by the classical music establishment. It was true of Copland, of the New England neoclassical school (Piston, Menin, Creston, Persichetti, and others), and of the minimalists (Glass, Reich, Riley, and their colleagues).

It's also important to distinguish between the academic serialists and the self-styled "avant-garde," a group of composers who often sound somewhat similar (frequently atonal), but whose philosophical underpinnings are quite different. This group asks the question made most famous by composers such as John Cage: "What is music anyway?" They experiment with noise, with unusual forms of notation, with electronics or microtonal intervals, and sometimes incorporate non-Western elements as well. Again, there's nothing inherently wrong with this, and there have been great composers working in this area, too. Four of the most famous (and worth getting to know) are Conlon Nancarrow, whose studies for player piano stand among the most remarkable of all twentieth-century works; Morton Feldman, who explores slowly evolving patterns over great spans of time at very low dynamic levels; George

Crumb, a true tone poet with an utterly personal style based on unusual playing techniques; and Charles Ives, whose music was popularized and championed by Leonard Bernstein.

Like the academic serialists, the twentieth-century avant-garde became institutionalized and fell victim to its pursuit of novelty for its own sake. I vividly recall a music history professor I once studied under, who as a composer wrote only works using graphic notation. When asked why, all he could say was that composing with the usual notes was no longer "valid," and anyone who disagreed with him was not worth speaking to. Needless to say, his oeuvre has remained cloaked in a richly earned obscurity from which it likely will never emerge. Ironically, the avant-garde is probably the most backward thinking of all of the modern compositional schools, because it depends on an evolutionary view of artistic progress rooted squarely in nineteenth-century romanticism, and in particular in Wagner's grandiose visions of "the music of the future."

It would be a mistake, however, to suggest that in bucking these trends Bernstein was alone. Far from it. The majority of twentieth-century composers in America and most other places have always worked within the tonal tradition, but aside from a few exceptions (Aaron Copland, for example; Dmitri Shostakovich; or the twentieth-century English school of Benjamin Britten, William Walton, and Ralph Vaughan Williams), these were not the figures whose work was most often recognized and performed. Until recently, the announcement of a modern novelty at a symphony concert was tantamount to telling the audience to get ready to suffer. But because he had a unique podium presence and opportunity to present his own works, Bernstein became something of a paradigm for the composer who represented the more reactionary, regressive elements in contemporary music. This view of him was tremendously unfair, as well as completely incorrect.

## Bernstein the Progressive

Even if we assume that atonality and other manifestations of the avant-garde mentality represent "progress" in a positive sense, they only do so in a very limited way. Specifically, for much of the nineteenth and twentieth centuries, progress in music was viewed largely in harmonic terms, whether this meant increasing use of dissonance and chromaticism such as we find in Wagner's *Tristan und Isolde*, the free atonality of Ives and the early works of the Second Viennese School, or the evolution of the twelve-tone (serial) system. But of course there are other ways of judging musical progress, and other developments equally important.

One of these was the emancipation of rhythm, perhaps best represented by the early ballets of Stravinsky (*The Firebird, Petrushka*, and above all, *The Rite of Spring*). It is very difficult to overestimate the importance of this innovation, because rhythm, used as an independent formal and structural element, not only imparts a sense of forward movement so crucial to the listener's perception of purposeful musical development, but it can function in this manner as a sort of replacement for classical tonality (exploiting the contrast between related keys), which fulfilled this same purpose. This permits the composer to write music with a relatively high level of tonal tension (dissonance), even to the point of atonality, or no dissonance at all, without giving the impression of formlessness and either irritating or boring the listener to death.

The exploitation of rhythm received further impetus from the influence of American popular music, jazz in particular. Very few twentieth-century composers of note failed to take advantage of this new and fertile source of musical material, particularly in France (Debussy and Ravel most famously). Bernstein belonged to the second generation of composers interested in these uniquely modern elements, and the fact that he was not an innovator in this regard hardly disqualifies him from being regarded as musically progressive. Moreover, he found himself in good company: Gershwin and Copland, of course, but also many other worthy composers such as (to name only a few) Ned Rorem, Morton Gould, David Diamond, Darius Milhaud, Randall Thompson, and Albert Roussel, all of whom Bernstein championed as a conductor. Most of these composers aren't generally regarded as major musical "progressives," but their music has endured and is still performed where so many more self-consciously avant-garde figures have faded from sight. Progressive or not, it is recognizably of the twentieth century, and so is Bernstein's music. It's also worth remembering in this connection that when his first major works began appearing in the early 1940s (the First Symphony dates from 1942), they were exactly contemporaneous with major concert pieces by Britten, Walton, Copland, Honegger, Messiaen, Prokofiev, Shostakovich, Martinů, Poulenc, Harris, and numerous other composers whose work has long been recognized as excellent as well as thoroughly modern.

Artists who are advanced for their time, and who have little else to offer, seldom remain appealing (or remain "advanced") in the estimation of later generations. They become yesterday's news. There is always a trendy new fashion on the horizon, and this year's revolution will be next year's orthodoxy. On the other hand, those who incorporate progressive elements into a wider aesthetic framework may achieve the sort of recognizable personal idiom that we value in assessing the importance of any composer. This is precisely the context in which Bernstein's work should be considered.

Furthermore, his approach has been triumphantly vindicated by the return to tonality and the unapologetically eclectic style of many of today's best American composers, from John Adams to Christopher Rouse, Michael Daugherty, and Jennifer Higdon. Seen from today's perspective, Bernstein's bold mixing of genres appears not just successful in terms of his own achievement, but prophetic of the actual direction that contemporary music seems to be taking. The vestiges of academic serialism and avant-garde effrontery will likely be with us for a while, but they are clearly on the losing side of history, just as Bernstein looks to be one of the winners.

## The Curse of Popularity

Writing a great tune is the Holy Grail of composition, and most composers know it. When Elgar was working on his "Pomp and Circumstance" March No. 1, the central trio section of which has since become famous as the "graduation march" for high schools and colleges the world over, he pulled his wife into his studio saying, "I've got a tune that will knock 'em flat!" There is no specific formula and no set of rules that determine what makes a melody memorable, affecting, inspiring, and distinctive, and the ability to write them is a gift. Bernstein had it, and he exercised it lavishly through his life.

Many of Bernstein's most famous tunes occur where you would most expect to find them: in the songs he wrote for his Broadway musicals, where they have since passed into the vernacular of twentieth-century popular music, including such hits as "Tonight" and "Maria" from *West Side Story*, "New York, New York" from *On the Town*, and "Glitter and Be Gay" from *Candide*. But the popular song style also permeates his concert works, ballets, and other pieces. Examples include the Danzón from the ballet *Fancy Free*, "God Said" from *Mass*, and the delicious "Turkey Trot" from the late *Divertimento* for orchestra.

This stylistic eclecticism, the free mixing of popular and more "serious" elements, has never gone over well in the elitist world of classical music scholarship and criticism. It was, in fact, exactly this alleged defect that dogged the music of Mahler for so many decades, and it is precisely this quality that drew Bernstein to his great predecessor's works in the first place. Bernstein always was a serious composer, if by this we mean one who understood how to find the right material for the right context, be it a popular tune or a theme capable of symphonic development. He understood the requirements of every genre in which he worked.

Through much of the latter half of the twentieth century, Bernstein was seen as the composer of a couple of very popular musicals who also had the temerity to work in larger, more ambitious genres. This view gets it backward. Bernstein was without question a composer of serious art music first, who also wrote for the musical theater. The distinction is an important one. His earliest compositions, if we exclude juvenilia, are mostly in large, abstract forms (see the works list at the end of this book): sonatas for piano, violin, and clarinet; a piano trio; and the First Symphony. Bernstein's talent for musical theater, evident since his youth, is merely one component of his larger genius for composition generally.

Nevertheless, whenever a composer writes a certifiable smash hit—and in *West Side Story* and *On the Town*, Bernstein delivered at least two—a couple of things inevitably happen. First, the popular successes overshadow everything else. It happened to Gustav Holst, for example, with his orchestral suite *The Planets*, and even to Vivaldi with *The Four Seasons* and Handel with *Messiah*. Popularity is usually synonymous with songs, a catchy tune, or at least a certain degree of brevity that encourages easy familiarity and discourages the need for time-consuming study and reflection. This is the price of fame, of becoming a name that even the casual music consumer recognizes. It's a price that most composers pay willingly.

Second, questions start to be asked about the nature of the successful composer's talent. Is he really a serious artist, or merely a hack tunesmith? Does he truly understand the demands of abstract music in large forms, and have any business attempting it? These aren't issues to be taken lightly. There is nothing wrong with trying to assess and evaluate any artist's ability to succeed at what he self-evidently attempts. Furthermore, all artists, if they are honest with themselves, have to grapple with these questions on a personal level. Bernstein, partly because of his career as a conductor and his attendant knowledge of so much earlier music, had a particularly acute awareness of his place in history, and of the possibilities and pitfalls awaiting the modern composer of serious classical music.

So there is a big difference between popularity and pandering, and between mindful versatility and mindless eclecticism. In short, Bernstein always knew exactly what he was doing. You may not always like it, but the reason will not stem from the composer's inability to find material appropriate to his artistic designs. Much of the more vocal criticism aimed at his most famous popular scores boils down to little more than professional jealousy and snobbery masquerading as "refined taste." The last thing the classical music establishment wants to admit is that sometimes the larger public gets it right and shows better artistic judgment than the professional tastemakers. Bernstein, like most great composers, cared about his audience, and wrote accordingly.

From the foregoing discussion, it is clear that Bernstein was a composer working largely in the grand tradition of Western, tonal classical music. His works contain traditional, popular, and progressive elements synthesized into an unmistakably original, personal idiom. Let's continue, then, by looking briefly at the most prominent ideas and characteristics running through his scores; for make no mistake, the better you get to know these pieces, the clearer it becomes that each belongs to a single, consistent, strikingly unified body of work.

## The Jewish Legacy

There were many fine twentieth-century Jewish composers, but only three major names whose Jewish faith and roots became an integral part of their musical language: Ernest Bloch, Arnold Schoenberg, and Leonard Bernstein. These three had very different styles. Schoenberg, of course, has already been mentioned, and one of his greatest masterpieces is the opera *Moses und Aron*, a gripping twelve-tone biblical drama. Schoenberg wrote other important "Jewish" works as well, including the harrowing *A Survivor from Warsaw*, and it may be no coincidence that these have become some of the composer's best-known vocal pieces.

Swiss-American composer Ernest Bloch (1880–1959) is best known today for his specifically "Jewish" works. These include the popular symphonic poem for cello and orchestra *Schelomo* (which Bernstein recorded twice), *Baal Shem, Three Jewish Poems, Voice in the Wilderness, Suite Hebraïque,* and the choral *Sacred Service* (which Bernstein also recorded). Bloch was an extremely accomplished composer who deserves far more attention than he usually gets. Part of the problem stems from the fact that he had several different styles, and anyone particularly fond of his Jewish idiom, which is basically a personal brand of the same romantic orientalism that we find in such popular works as Rimsky-Korsakov's *Scheherazade*, probably won't like Bloch's more abstract (and difficult) chamber and orchestral pieces.

Bernstein's Jewish faith was tremendously important to him both personally and as an integral component of his musical voice. Unlike Schoenberg, whose musical evolution and choice of idiom operated independently of his subject matter, or Bloch, who adapted a preexisting romantic melodic and harmonic vocabulary to his personal needs, Bernstein incorporated real Jewish liturgical elements into a number of his compositions. Specifically, anyone who has attended a Jewish service and heard a reading of the Torah (the first five books of the

Bible) will have encountered some of the basic melodic materials that inspired Bernstein.

We'll have much more to say about this in considering the individual pieces, but for now suffice it to say that Bernstein's "Jewish" works comprise arguably the most important single group in his entire output, including the First and Third symphonies, *Halil* for flute and orchestra, *Chichester Psalms*, the ballet *Dybbuk*, and large chunks of both *Mass* and the Concerto for Orchestra. Because this list includes many of Bernstein's largest and most complex pieces, it goes without saying that his Jewish works are not, with the exception of the ebullient *Chichester Psalms*, necessarily his easiest and most popular. To understand why, we turn to the next element in Bernstein personal musical makeup.

## The Crisis of Faith

Many composers have certain philosophical or aesthetic concerns that permeate their work. Benjamin Britten, for example, was often obsessed with the theme of innocence corrupted. Puccini's famous "little girls" (Mimi in *La bohème*, Cio-Cio-San in *Madama Butterfly*, Liù in *Turandot*) love unreservedly, then suffer and die for their troubles. Bernstein's Jewishness was not a blind faith; rather, a probing, doubt-filled striving to believe despite the horrors of the two world wars and the ensuing cold war threat of nuclear annihilation. He challenges openly man's faith in God, in himself, and by implication the rationality of the belief in God's covenant. These are not easy questions, and despite what his detractors might say, Bernstein offers no easy answers.

Much of the music in which he grapples with these issues, aside from its ready accessibility, is traumatic, though sometimes ultimately cathartic. Not all of it ends happily. Although for the most part optimistic by nature, and joyous, even celebratory in expression, Bernstein's art (as we will see) remains true to its subject, and pursues its designs to their logical conclusions. Both the "Kaddish" Symphony (No. 3) and *Mass* take the general shape of a religious celebration gone wrong; the mere recitation of holy words cannot hide the emptiness felt by those doing the reciting. This leads to total emotional collapse, out of which faith is slowly restored.

The First Symphony ("Jeremiah") has a slow, somber finale for mezzo-soprano and orchestra, setting carefully chosen extracts (in Hebrew) from the prophet's biblical lamentations. The plot of the ballet *Dybbuk* is frankly creepy but quite wonderful: a tale of Kabbalah, mysticism, and demonic possession in a Hasidic Jewish community. This battle between good and evil, symbolized by the contrast between tonal and atonal musical idioms, ends equivocally, as you will soon see. *West Side Story* is that rare phenomenon, a musical comedy with a tragic conclusion. The ballet *Facsimile* is a study in human relationships that fail to connect in a meaningful way.

## Love

You might argue that these latter two works are not explicitly religious, but the crisis of faith in Bernstein's world, as just suggested, is not just about God and religion. It also concerns man's inhumanity to man (a point made explicit in the Third Symphony's spoken text), and ordinary people's need to find love and believe in each other. Bernstein's most notable essay on the theme of love is his *Serenade* for violin and orchestra after Plato's *Symposium*, which is also one of his very greatest works in any form. It's also important to bear in mind that love's agonies—its "crisis of faith" aspects—are but one of the aspects that Bernstein consistently explores, and by no means the most significant.

Bernstein was keenly aware also of love's pleasures, and of its potential for happiness and humor. It's worth keeping in mind the old saying that there are only two real operatic plots: Two people fall in love and get married, or they fall in love and both of them die. Bernstein's music, with its often extreme contrasts between giddy high spirits and emotional desolation, certainly understands this. Like Mahler, he was not afraid to risk triviality to explore territory sometimes considered unworthy of a "serious" composer, and in his music as in his person he was always fond of a good joke, and appreciative of life's little ironies.

I can speak of this last quality at first hand, and would like to take a moment to pass on to posterity a little tidbit of Bernstein lore. When he was in London in the late 1980s for the series of concert performances of *Candide* that would culminate in the Deutsche Grammophon recording and video, my younger sister was studying there for a semester. Her roommate was singing in the chorus. Everyone was sick, not the least Bernstein, who was suffering from the flu. My sister managed to get into one of the rehearsals with another roommate (who captured as a memento of the occasion a terrific photo of Bernstein's nose). She very much wanted to get me his autograph. So she ran across the street to a nearby bookstore to get one of Bernstein's books for him to sign.

The only thing she could find was Joan Peyser's scandal-mongering unauthorized "biography" (I use the term advisedly), a mean-spirited hatchet job that had caused Bernstein no little embarrassment. Whether or not she was aware of the furor that the book had caused, my sister bought it and presented it to a sick and hoarse Bernstein for signature. "It's for my brother," she said, "he's a music critic." "Well," Bernstein replied, "it's probably a good idea to stay on the good side of the critics." And sign it he did. On the off chance that it might become a collector's item as the only autographed copy of Peyser's biography, I donated it to the New York Philharmonic archive a few years ago so that it could be preserved properly.

We find this lighter side of Bernstein's character most tellingly displayed, obviously, in the musical comedies, *On the Town, Wonderful Town, Candide*, and even *West Side Story*—despite the tragic ending. In his music Bernstein was, among his other qualities, genuinely witty. It's one of the reasons he was such a great Haydn conductor. His sense of fun is also evident in such works as the ballet *Fancy Free*, the *Divertimento*, the *Serenade* just mentioned, and in shorter works such as *Slava!* and *A Musical Toast*, affectionate tributes to friends and colleagues. Perhaps it helps to think of Bernstein's music in its broadest sense of being about relationships, both personal and spiritual, and this accounts for much of its expressive range and immediate impact.

There is one other story I would like to share with you that speaks directly to the question of love in Bernstein's character, and much as I prefer to let each musical work speak for itself, there's something here that strikes me as particularly touching and relevant. Just how credible the episode is you can judge for yourself, but I have no reason to doubt its authenticity. It has the ring of truth, and in a performing arts world that thrives on gossip, much of it malicious, perhaps this conversation will serve as timely corrective. All of the participants are gone now, and nothing here reflects poorly on any of them.

The late Antonio de Almeida was a fine conductor with unusually broad musical tastes and a vast number of friends and acquaintances in the classical music world. It was an honor for me to be one of them. Another, going back many years, was Leonard Bernstein, who lent his support to one of Almeida's particular musical passions, the "Friends of French Opera" association. He had met Bernstein as a student at Tanglewood, the Boston Symphony's summer home and music school, which had been founded by the great conductor (and Bernstein's mentor) Serge Koussevitzky. Tony (as his friends called him), who was French-Portuguese, was also friendly with Bernstein's wife, the Chilean actress Felicia Montealegre.

The couple's sometimes stormy relationship has been explored at length elsewhere, and there's no need to recapitulate that particular tale here. Almeida happened to see Montealegre at a time when her marriage was under particular strain as a result of Bernstein's widely publicized gay affairs. As he recounted the conversation to me, Tony at one point asked her, "Why do you put up with his behavior? How can you stand it?" She replied, "Tony, he has so much love to give, and I know that he has so much love for me that even if I can't have it all, it's enough."

Some might view Montealegre's words as sad, but that was not how she meant them, or how Tony understood them in the context that he quoted them to me. Artists, particularly in the classical music business, are often notoriously catty in talking about each other, often out of jealousy or just plain resentment. Tony wasn't. He was a gentleman, as well as a great admirer of Bernstein. One of the qualities he valued most in the man and his music was the uninhibited abundance of love that characterized both.

It is depressing to see theoretically objective Bernstein scholarship come to the conclusion, because his sexual orientation was basically gay, that he must have gotten married to further his career, or because it was expected at the time, or to please his mentor Serge Koussevitzky, or for any one of a number of reasons save the single one that makes the most sense: that he loved, really loved, Felicia Montealegre, just as he loved the children that they raised together. Bernstein also loved his friends, his wider family, and his audience, each in their own way. This sort of "zero sum game" theorizing about emotions, in which feelings of one kind necessarily preclude feelings of another, really says much more about Bernstein's biographers than it does about the man.

The point of this story, then, is not to sanitize Bernstein's image, or to suggest that the behavior of this incredibly complex man didn't inflict pain on those around him. His own children have described eloquently the traumatic period in which their parents separated, their mother was diagnosed with terminal lung cancer, and Bernstein ultimately returned to her, guilt-ridden, before the end. But his sometimes questionable behavior towards his family doesn't mean that his love wasn't genuine. Like most self-absorbed artists, Bernstein's actions didn't always reflect well on him. Being a genius didn't make him perfect. In that respect at least he was no better, and maybe in some ways worse, than the rest of us. What does make him different, though, is his ability to express and share his feelings of love through his music.

## The Primacy of Melody

In Bernstein's music tonal melody represents a basic affirmation of faith, often appearing as the outcome of conflict between tonal and atonal elements (as in the ballet *Dybbuk*, the Third Symphony, *Halil* for flute and orchestra, or in sections of *Mass*.) This reflects a profound insight into the basic nature of Western music because tunes, however stylized, all have their origins in the human singing voice. In turning its back on melody, much twentieth-century music (in Bernstein's view) also lost its faith in humanity; it ceased to express human feeling and human aspiration. Bernstein's music, whether or not aided by a text, rejects this notion categorically.

Much of the theoretical discussion that characterized the battle between tonal and atonal music in the latter half of the twentieth century was purely technical. It suited the cause of the academic serialists to frame the debate as a conflict between two compositional systems, one contemporary, the other obsolete, neither having any intrinsic superiority. This of course ignores the crucial fact that for most listeners tonal music *means* something, whereas purely atonal music, absent contrasting tonal elements, does not. And whenever those contrasting tonal elements are indeed present, the emotions expressed by the atonal bits are usually perceived as negative, miserable, painful, or even evil.

Bernstein explored this issue at some length in his series of Harvard lectures, later published (and filmed) as *The Unanswered Question*. For most of human history it has been accepted without question that music is a language that speaks of feelings and emotions, and the bearer of meaning is *melody*. Whether this construct is right or wrong in any objective sense really isn't important. That fact is that Bernstein was a terrific composer of tunes, and anyone with that gift would be a fool not to exploit it to the full. The sad irony is that classical music in the twentieth century had gotten itself into such a state that a great melodist who was also a serious composer effectively had to apologize for exploiting his own talent to best effect.

It's still too seldom noted what an original tunesmith Bernstein was. Throughout much of the nineteenth century, romantic composers defined themselves through their personal melodic style: Think of such names as Tchaikovsky, Dvořák, Sibelius, Wagner, and Verdi, composers whose works are immediately identifiable from just a few seconds of melody. Twentieth-century atonal composers didn't have to worry about tunes in the traditional sense, and the most famous of the (mostly) tonal composers, Igor Stravinsky, borrowed many of his from elsewhere. Copland's most popular melody, "Simple Gifts," isn't by Copland at all.

Even now, when the return to tonality has become an accepted practice, many composers either borrow individual melodies or construct musical collages out of different, preexisting thematic elements (an approach pioneered by Charles Ives in the early 1900s). Composers who write completely original tunes are vanishingly rare. Francis Poulenc was one, and Bernstein was another. Although he very occasionally will borrow a theme from an earlier classic, such as the reference to the finale of Mendelssohn's Violin Concerto in the third act of *A Quiet Place*, or the Hasidic music in *Dybbuk*, the overwhelming majority of the material that he employs is custom made.

There's also remarkably little borrowing from one work to the next, though there is some, the most obvious example being the opera *Trouble in Tahiti*, which became most of the second act of its sequel, *A Quiet Place*. Even the ballet *Fancy Free* and the musical *On the Town*, the latter of which grew out of the ballet and not only deals with the same plot (three sailors on shore leave) but contains a substantial dance component, share nothing significant thematically. So if Bernstein cannot be said to stake a significant claim to originality as a musical modernist, he certainly does so in terms of sheer inspiration. We have no way to put a value on the amount of effort that goes into creating distinctive melodic material for each new work, but if we could then Bernstein's compositional genius would be far more readily acclaimed.

Although he wrote tunes of every conceivable emotional stripe, the one characteristic that they all share, if I had to sum it up in one word, is elegance. There's a gracefulness and fluidity to Bernstein's melodies, a rhythmic lift that makes them special. This explains his success as a composer for the ballet, but also the energetic impulse behind such hit tunes as "Tonight" from *West Side Story*, or the sweetly winsome theme that appears midway through the central movement of the "Jeremiah" Symphony. All of this is quintessential Bernstein, and we'll take particular care in the discussions of the individual works to point out these special moments whenever they appear.

## Latin Rhythms

One really important aspect of Bernstein's musical makeup that has received remarkably little attention is his absorption of Latino/Hispanic elements into his own personal language. Of course, everyone points to the Puerto Rican music in *West Side Story* (which is actually more Mexican, if you want to get technical) as a prime example of Bernstein using an ethnic idiom to inject some local color into a theatrical work, but the truth is that the impact of this music on him was much more profound and pervasive than that. Today, when Latin popular music is all the rage, it's easy to forget that this really represents a sort of second wave of cultural influence. In the 1940s and '50s, Mexican, Cuban, and Brazilian dance and club music was if anything even more novel, and certainly more exotic, than much of what we find now.

The first wave of Latin influence represented a counterbalance to traditional European models in both popular and classical music. In the pop world, we need only think of "lounge music" icons such as Esquivel, or the character of Ricky Ricardo in the television series *I Love Lucy*. In the classical music world, composers such as Carlos Chavez, Heitor Villa-Lobos, George Gershwin, Morton Gould, and Aaron Copland exploited Latin American musical idioms with relish. Bernstein participated fully in this trend, and it was in this environment that his own personal voice came to maturity. The reason that this element tends to be downplayed in discussion of his work, it would seem, has to do with the problems some musical scholars have in dealing with popular music generally, as well as a tendency to view this eclecticism of Bernstein's as a weakness rather than a strength.

His love of Latin culture also had a purely personal foundation in the person of Mrs. Bernstein herself, who was not only Chilean but also quite musical. While the biographical literature naturally spends a great deal of time speculating and commenting on the personal aspects of Bernstein's relationship to his wife, there seems to be very little discussion of her possible influence on his creative work as a musician, an influence that strikes me as very pertinent, and very real. It's a subject that certainly warrants serious investigation from someone qualified to evaluate all of the musical evidence, and to maintain the necessary degree of objectivity in evaluating the complex relationship between these two very strong-willed people.

For our purposes, suffice it to say that the most obvious Latin American influence on Bernstein's music concerns his treatment of rhythm. It gives his music its bounce and lift, a result of its pervasive fondness for irregular (five or seven beats per measure) and compound meters (that is, rhythms that can alternate freely between two and three beats per measure). The most famous example of this is the song "America" from *West Side Story*, where each line of the refrain, starting with "I like to be in America" and comprising two measures of music, has the following rhythmic accent in 6/8 time. As you can see and hear, the rhythm switches from 2x3 (eighth notes) to 3x2 (quarter notes) from the first measure to the second, in an exciting combination of forward momentum and emphatic accents:

| Note value: | 1/8 | 1/8 | 1/8 | 1/8 | 1/8 | 1/8 | 1/4 | 1/4 | 1/4 |
|---|---|---|---|---|---|---|---|---|---|
| | I | like | to | BE | In | A | ME | RI | CA |
| Rhythm: | 1 | 2 | 3 | 4 | 5 | 6 | 1 2 | 3 4 | 5 6 |

However, this treatment of rhythm goes far beyond those moments where Bernstein is pretending to be Puerto Rican. It permeates much of his quicker music, including such abstract pieces as the central movement of the "Jeremiah" Symphony and almost the entirety of *A Musical Toast*, as well as one of the principal numbers in *Songfest* and a great deal of the ballet music—mostly famously, the Danzón in *Fancy Free*. The Latin beat not only energizes the music's textures, it helps (along with the equally pervasive jazz element) to give it a typically "American" sound: crisp, sophisticated, and sexy without turning merely sentimental.

## Formal Mastery

Most discussions of form in music approach the subject either wholly technically or, when writing in a more popular vein, with great trepidation. This is a pity, because it's a fascinating subject and all music, even the simplest song, has a distinctive form that listeners comprehend instinctively. Bernstein's approach to form was highly original, and as personal as his melodic sense. For example, none of his three symphonies follows the traditional, four-movement structure of opening quick movement, slow movement, scherzo (dance movement), and quick finale, and yet each is unquestionably "symphonic" in its handling of themes, and in charting a clear emotional trajectory, forging unity out of a diverse range of material.

The First Symphony ("Jeremiah") adopts a slow-fast-slow, three movement form, and concludes with an extended solo for mezzo-soprano. Symphony No. 2 ("The Age of Anxiety," after the W. H. Auden poem of the same name) contains a concerto-like ("concertante") piano solo, and has a completely original structure inspired by, but not unmusically bound to, the literary text. The Third Symphony ("Kaddish") is a melodrama, a work for speaker and orchestra with a substantial choral contribution as well, that also weaves the four movements of the traditional symphony into a continuous whole.

Similarly, although Bernstein wrote no pieces that he called "concerto," his *Serenade* is unquestionably a violin concerto, whereas *Halil* is a flute concerto. When he employs traditional forms: sonata, theme and variations, prelude and fugue—all of which will be discussed and explained as necessary—he does so in fresh and interesting ways. He was always concerned with giving his works a clear and distinctive shape. Even his ballets, traditionally a somewhat fragmentary medium, work unusually well as concert pieces. The subtitle of *Facsimile*, a "Choreographic Essay," explicitly asks us to consider the formal element. It's no mistake that the arrangement he made of his single film score *On the Waterfront* is called a *Symphonic* Suite, or that the orchestral excerpts from *West Side Story* are known as *Symphonic* Dances.

Bernstein's handling of form tends to be dynamic; that is, the thematic material dictates the shape of the work. He does not simply pour new wine into old bottles, as was the case with so much second rate music in the romantic period. Both Bernstein's conducting and his own music are so emotionally expressive that the care he lavished on sculpting the formal element and making it readily audible to the listener often goes unnoticed. Certainly this was frequently the case looking back on the critical reaction to his music making, but I can attest personally to how important this aspect of his art was to him.

Back around 1987, when I was just starting out as a music critic for *High Fidelity* magazine, I was asked to review Bernstein's Deutsche Grammophon recording of Tchaikovsky's Sixth Symphony

("Pathétique"). Bernstein's late recordings were controversial on account of their extremely slow tempos in the (already) slow movements, and this one was no exception. The work's despairing finale, which usually plays for about nine or ten minutes, stretched out to nearly double that. Many critics were infuriated, and dismissed the performance as a typical example of Bernstein's penchant for emotional indulgence and lack of self-discipline.

I heard the performance somewhat differently. In my view, the unprecedented emotional intensity of the finale arose from a careful rethinking of the entire work, and from Bernstein's attempt to create an expressive equilibrium between the very long and dramatic first movement and the complete surrender to despair that characterizes the finale. The result was a last movement that approached the first in length. It may not be to everyone's taste, but the point seemed to me very clear. Anyway, after the review was published, I got a call from my editor, who told me that Bernstein had asked his secretary to convey his personal thanks for the review because it had in fact correctly understood and described his intentions.

Sharing this story, admittedly, risks sounding like an exercise in self-promotion, but it does put some flesh on the discussion, and hopefully will allow you to listen to Bernstein's music with a keener awareness of an element on which he devoted much thought. In all great music, form serves to focus and channel emotional expression; and the more effective the composer's feeling for structure, the more intense and powerful the end result will be. So if you find Bernstein's music particularly gripping and affecting, one of the main reasons, whether you are conscious of it or not, will be his ability to give each work, and each section within it, a fully satisfying shape.

## Theatricality

Most of Bernstein's music was in fact written for the theater, but that's not quite the same as calling it "theatrical." The very term is somewhat vague, and not always complimentary. If you look it up in a dictionary (and I just did on dictionary.com), you may find among its several definitions the following: "suggestive of the theater or of acting; artificial, pompous, spectacular, or extravagantly histrionic." So we must use the word with care and specificity, for Bernstein's music is never artificial. But like any good actor, it has the ability to convincingly evoke any emotion or feeling, and the uninhibited and (yes) "extravagantly histrionic" way in which it does so often comes across as, at the very least, larger than life.

Some people find this embarrassing, which is curious, particularly in the world of modern classical music. In England, for example, composers such as Britten, Tippett, and more recently Thomas Adès (in the nymphomaniac opera *Powder Her Face*) have dealt with some frighteningly crass or sensitive subjects, and set some hair-raisingly awful texts, without ever having their basic seriousness questioned. Next to them, Bernstein seems the very soul of discretion. Besides, when I speak of his music's theatricality, I am thinking not so much of his music for the stage; rather, of how his music comes across in the concert hall.

For example, Bernstein was, among other things, a very fine pianist. He successfully recorded concertos by Ravel, Shostakovich, and Mozart, and sometimes accompanied singers in recital. The piano was *his* instrument, and it often features prominently as a sort of musical protagonist in his orchestral works, including the ballets *Fancy Free, Facsimile,* and the Second Symphony. Of all the abstract musical forms, the concerto, with its origins in the operatic aria, is the most theatrical, a contest of wills between soloist and the larger ensemble. It may seem doubly curious, then, that Bernstein wrote no avowed concertos, but this evident oddity resolves itself if we note that whatever it happens to be called, very few of his works are free of either concertante elements or actual singing.

The opposition to programmatic or narrative elements in supposedly abstract instrumental music has its origins in the nineteenth-century battle between Liszt and Wagner on the one hand, as the proponents of "new music," and Brahms on the other, as the upholder of "classical" ideals. That this antiquated aesthetic dispute still colors our view of contemporary music now and then may seem more than a bit demented—and so it is, but it's there all the same. None of Bernstein's music is "pure" in the sense that those opposed to theatricality usually mean. Indeed, neither was Brahms's or any other Western composer's after about the sixteenth century.

The issue with Bernstein, though, is that most composers writing in supposedly abstract large forms, such as symphonies and concertos, aren't anxious to advertise their theatricality, whereas Bernstein revels in his. In the preface to the score of his Second Symphony, he comes straight out and says, "If the charge of 'theatricality' in a symphonic work is a valid one, I am willing to plead guilty. I have a deep suspicion that every work I write, for whatever medium, is really theater music in some way . . ."

Issues of time and opportunity aside, it may be that this accounts for the relative dearth of chamber music in Bernstein's output, or even of solo works for his own instrument, the piano. He needed the larger canvas of the orchestra on which to work, with its bold contrasts, vibrant coloristic resources, and the potential for musical characterization—all of which brings us to our last point:

# Joy

There are few artists about whom the word *joy* comes up as frequently as it does in connection with Bernstein—the man, the conductor, and the composer. The word appears in the title of his most popular book, *The Joy of Music*, and it's suggested by another: *The Infinite Variety of Music*. And with joy, comes pleasure. We began by citing mezzo-soprano Christa Ludwig on the subject of Bernstein's genius, and it's fitting to close with her words as well:

> I was raised to regard music as something sacred, but from Bernstein, I learned about its joys and pleasures. Suddenly I felt music more fully, and discovered that it had another dimension. After working with Bernstein, music was for me deeper, higher, wider. It entered deeply into every part of my being.

Here, then, is Bernstein's art in a nutshell: an exploration of the crisis of faith and the difficulties in achieving meaningful relationships, everywhere and always counterbalanced by the certainty of love, joy, and pleasure in life, and also naturally in music. Bernstein's works are about people and for people; they are humane, caring, vivid, and full of fun. Listen, and enjoy.

# Symphonies and Concertos

F or Bernstein, to write a symphony meant to deal with important issues, and all three of his works in that genre address matters of special significance to him: the crisis of faith and the need for people for forge meaningful relationships among themselves and with their Creator. In this sense, Bernstein's conception of the symphony was romantic and heroic, but his handling of the actual musical material was fresh, modern, and new. In his concerted works for solo and orchestra, on the other hand, the overt references to external programs are less obvious, and the music is more "abstract." This is true even of the Violin Concerto (a.k.a. the *Serenade*), nominally inspired by Plato's *Symposium*. At all times, however, the formal inventiveness remains very striking. Together, these works offer a complete portrait of Bernstein the man and musician. They are true musical landmarks.

## Symphony No. 1 ("Jeremiah") (1942)

*Scoring: piccolo, 2 flutes, 2 oboes, English horn, E-flat clarinet,*
   *2 clarinets, bass clarinet, 2 bassoons, contrabassoon, 4 horns,*
   *3 trumpets, 3 trombones, tuba, snare drum, bass drum,*
   *cymbals, triangle, wood block, maracas, timpani, piano,*
   *mezzo-soprano solo, and strings*

It may seem strange to begin this discussion of Bernstein's First Symphony talking about a work by another composer, but some-times the best way to provide a context for understanding is to make comparisons, and here we have a particularly useful one. Benjamin Britten's *Sinfonia da requiem* dates from exactly the same period as Bernstein's First Symphony. It was written in 1940 and premiered by the New York Philharmonic under John Barbirolli at Carnegie Hall in 1941. A performance by Bernstein's mentor Serge Koussevitzky took place in Boston a year later, the same year that Bernstein completed his First Symphony (which he had begun in 1939 by composing the lament that later became its finale). The Boston performance led Koussevitzky to award Britten a commission for an opera, *Peter Grimes*, the work that put twentieth-century English opera on the map, and which had an American premiere at Tanglewood conducted by none other than Leonard Bernstein.

Bernstein's symphony, though completed in 1942, was first performed in 1944 by the Pittsburgh Symphony, followed by another performance in Boston. By this time Bernstein had already made his now legendary appearance as conductor of the New York Philharmonic, stepping in for an indisposed Bruno Walter. Britten's work is dedicated to the memory of his parents; Bernstein's, to his father (who was very much alive at the time; he passed away in 1969). Both symphonies have three movements played without pause, the first of which is a passionate threnody, the second a sort of danse macabre based on folk music (Britten uses an Irish jig, Bernstein borrows Jewish liturgical motives), and both end in a state of uneasy calm. Both pieces reflect their composers' reaction to the outbreak of the Second World War.

Additionally, the first movements of the two symphonies feature ominous drum beats that recur periodically as a sort of leitmotif. The Wagnerian term *leitmotif* is appropriate, as an obvious point of reference is the timpani-laden "Siegfried's Funeral Music" from the German composer's epic *Götterdämmerung*. The point in making this observation is not to suggest that Bernstein copied Britten (not that it matters particularly, anyway). The origins of "Jeremiah" predate the completion of Britten's symphony, and even if the two composers were in contact during this period the differences between the two pieces are equally striking. Most obviously, Bernstein's symphony includes a vocal finale of singularly tragic character, whereas Britten's remains purely instrumental and expressively more consoling.

Even more significantly, Bernstein's work reveals him to be, first and foremost, a melodist, and a very great one at that. Britten, for all his compositional genius, did not build his reputation on the creation of memorable tunes, nor was he able to fuse popular and serious musical idioms in the effortless way typical of Bernstein. There's no question that the "Jeremiah" Symphony is a major achievement for a young composer of just twenty-four. It reveals an artist in full command of his personal idiom, and it inaugurates Bernstein's "miracle decade" as both a conductor and composer. In addition to "Jeremiah," the 1940s would see the birth of many of the works on which his reputation now rests: the musical *On the Town*, the ballets *Fancy Free* and *Facsimile*, the *Prelude, Fugue and Riffs*, and, closing out the decade, the Second Symphony.

## GUIDE TO LISTENING

One of the most remarkable facts about Bernstein's symphonies, formally speaking, is that none of them feature a movement in what traditionalists call *sonata form*. By this we mean a system of large scale tonal organization consisting of an *exposition* that presents the main themes of the movement in contrasting keys, a *development* that subjects them to a (hopefully) dramatic series of variations and combinations on the way to the *recapitulation*, or restatement of the initial material recomposed so as to emphasize the return to the movement's initial key. You may not consider this a big deal, but it really is because tonal instrumental music that wants to "go somewhere" or give the impression of "doing something," including most large works from the classical period onward, finds in sonata form a very natural, convenient, and effective method of achieving this goal.

No one was more aware of this than Bernstein. Indeed, so profound was his understanding of the issues involved in generating the kind of dynamic momentum critical to sustaining a successful symphonic structure, that he was able to look beyond the textbook version of sonata form (as just described) and instead get directly to the heart of the matter, what we might call the *sonata principle*, just as the great classical masters did. If this sounds complicated, and it in technical terms it truly is, there's no need to worry. What it means is that Bernstein's handling of tonality and his treatment of dissonance and modulation (moving from one key to another) are designed to produce a sense of movement, of tension and release, of struggle to reach a destination that seems in retrospect to have been preordained.

Simply put, Bernstein's symphonic music is never dull. It has no dead spots, no unnecessary padding, and follows an inner logic that's never incompatible with the music's expressive point. That he was able to achieve this in totally different ways, formally speaking, in his three symphonies really does stand as a remarkable achievement, and it is one that you can hear for yourself very easily. It also makes describing his instrumental works a relatively straightforward process, because all they ask is that you listen from point to point and let the music "do its thing." There's virtually no need to resort to specialized technical jargon, beyond those terms that most music lovers will encounter in the normal course of listening to the classics. The "Jeremiah" Symphony offers a case in point.

## First Movement: "Prophecy" (CD Track 1)

The symphony opens largamente ("broadly") with a dissonant, throbbing rhythm in two-note beats for strings and timpani. This ominous gesture of warning returns throughout the movement. A solo horn then states the principal motive out of which Bernstein generates the melody of the movement's first big section. Notice also the woodwinds' answer to the horn theme (backed by a gentle tap on the triangle). In the work's first bars, Bernstein has already opened up a sonic panorama beginning in the lowest register of the basses and extending upward to the highest notes of the piccolo. Not only does this bespeak the writing of a natural orchestral composer, it creates a dynamic "groping towards the light" that serves as an organizing principal for the work as a whole, characterizing each movement even though they do not share themes in a substantive way (with one major exception we'll discuss in its place).

For the first two and a half minutes, Bernstein spins out a yearning, stressful melody that evolves out of the opening horn motive. Higher and higher it climbs, only to be undermined by two-note "warning" gestures from the brass and timpani. At 2:43 it subsides into a soft transition for low clarinets and solemn brass, leading to a new, wistful melody for flutes and piccolo over a rhythmic string accompaniment built out of the two-note warning motive. Both the texture and the character of this theme (Bernstein marks it "very calm") bear a striking resemblance to the second subject in the first movement of Shostakovich's Fifth Symphony, a work then only a few years old, and one that Bernstein conducted often and extremely well.

Pay particular attention to the entrance of the divided violins at 4:38 with an expressive, pleading theme, immediately interrupted by those ubiquitous warning beats, rising swiftly to a powerful climax and initiating the return of the violin's initial melody. From this point the tension ebbs away into a softly pensive chord on muted lower strings (violas, cellos, and basses), that Bernstein directs should be held until just before the start of the next movement. When I spoke of Bernstein's ability to generate symphonic momentum in his music, consider that this opening has lasted about seven and a half minutes in slow tempo, but you may well find yourself amazed on reaching the end that the time has passed so quickly. The music has incredible energy; it surges.

## Second Movement: "Profanation" (CD Track 2)

Now comes the fun part. As anyone who has read Dante's *Divine Comedy* will tell you, hell is so much more entertaining the heaven. This wicked scherzo starts with out with a woodwind melody built out of the biblical tropes, or melodic cells that every Jewish kid learns as part of Bar Mitzvah practice. I did it, Bernstein did it, and while for non-Jews the result is wonderfully jazzy and exotic, for us members of the tribe the music always provides an extra kick and even a laugh. Of course, few things can be more profane than "jazzifying" the ancient melodies used to chant the Torah, so to that extent Bernstein has fulfilled his intentions in the music's first two seconds. The constantly shifting rhythms (6/8, 8/8, 6/8, 7/8, and 6/8 in the first seven bars alone) give the movement a deliciously off-kilter jolt as it proceeds.

Formally speaking this movement is a scherzo and trio. Traditionally scherzos, like the classical minuets the preceded them, take the following shape: AABB–Trio: CCDD–AB. Bernstein's is a bit different. He does give us a literal repeat of the scherzo's first half, its A section, but B is an extended development of the motives of the first part, and this again goes a long way toward giving the music that essential, goal-directed, symphonic substance without relaying on textbook notions of form. For example, check out the perky version of the opening theme that appears at 2:21 in the oboes and bassoons, or the big band version of the same tune for full orchestra at 2:55.

The trio, or middle section, begins at exactly 3:00 and does not follow the "two halves, both repeated" traditional form at all. It has three main ideas. The first is the menacing tune on the woodwinds in Latin rhythm that leads it off (call it C). Next comes a joyous little fanfare in the flutes (D), and then the Big Tune (E), one of the those effortlessly elegant, lyrical ideas that adorn Bernstein's ballets and musical theater works (and much else besides). It sails in at 3:23. The remainder of the trio follows the order: C–E(winds)–E(strings)–C–D(climactic brass and percussion)–C. I describe this section in so much detail because it really is marvelous to hear how Bernstein juggles these various tunes and motives as the music hurtles onward with uninterrupted thrust. Also, you may notice that E actually contains, within its second limb, a particularly graceful transformation of C. This is true symphonic writing.

A final appearance of the original C leads back to the scherzo proper, not softly, as it initially appeared, but from its first loud outburst, now amplified even further with plenty of assistance from the percussion. This recapitulation turns out to be greatly abbreviated and it contains a huge dramatic surprise, for just as it seems to be heading toward the expected vicious climax the little fanfare theme (D) from the trio section blasts in triumphantly (at 6:06) on the trumpets, urged on by timpani beaten with maracas (that's the clicking rhythm you hear underneath—a splendid effect). It's sort of the musical equivalent of the good guys escaping from captivity at the last minute, ankle chains clanking as they attempt to break free, but unfortunately the celebration turns out to be short lived.

The opening theme returns loudly in the horns, ushering in the trumpet and timpani-led climax that the outburst of D ostensibly supplanted, and with a few curt gestures the music slams to a brutal close.

Trust me when I tell you (speaking as a percussionist) that this piece is as much fun to play as it is to listen to. Indeed, it's such a thrill that there's a tendency to forget all about the fact that it's supposed to represent something nasty going on. In this respect, there is in Bernstein a great deal of Mozart's aesthetic dictum when he said, speaking of a scene from *The Abduction from the Seraglio*, that no matter how terrible the situation being the described, the music must never merely offend the ear. It must always remain captivating, and so it is here.

### Third Movement: "Lamentation" (CD Track 3)

Following is my own paraphrase in plain English of the Hebrew text from the Book of Lamentations. The translation supplied with the score is grotesque (for example the last line reads, "Turn Thou us unto Thee, O Lord," whatever that bit of mangled syntax means). If it's King James, or some other famous version, then the translator evidently was having a bad day. The slow finale starts immediately, with the entrance of the mezzo-soprano declaiming the following text in the original Hebrew, "tragically," as the score instructs. The voice is very discreetly accompanied. Listen to how much intensity Bernstein wrings from a simple sustained sixth in the violins, *forte*, accompanying the start of the second verse (at 0:50).

> 1:1–3
>
> How the city that was full of people sits alone! How she has become a widow! She who was once great among the nations, and a princess in the provinces; how she has become a tributary.
>
> She weeps in the night. Her tears run down her cheeks, and there is no one to comfort her among all of her lovers. All her friends have betrayed her, and have become enemies.
>
> Judah went into exile because of suffering and servitude. She now lives among the nations and finds no rest. Her pursuers caught up with her within the borders.

A gentle flute solo leads to consoling chords in the lower strings ("with great simplicity"), before the soloist intones the next line of text (at 2:57).

1:8

Jerusalem has sinned terribly.

The orchestra then continues alone, rising to a passionate climax capped by a crash from cymbals and bass drum, until at 4:43 the solo enters once again, *pianissimo*, "without rhythm and without warmth," with the remainder of the verse.

How the city sits alone . . . a widow.

At this point, (5:03), the flutes begin to draw the threads of the work together. The pleading motive from the first movement (CD Track 1, 4:38) enters timidly but brightly, another aspect of that "groping for the light" so fundamental to the music's message. As with most repetition in this symphony, the quotation isn't literal, but although modified the reference is clear. This develops with increasing passion, leading to the movement's dramatic climax, as the soloist sings:

4:14–15

They wander in the streets like blind men, polluted with blood so that men cannot touch their clothing.

"Depart, unclean!" they cried to them. "Depart, depart, and do not touch them!"

At the peak of intensity (7:27), as the mezzo-soprano hurls out her accusation, *fortissimo*, the brass recall the two-note "warning" from the very start of the symphony, and another cymbal-capped climax ushers in the first movement's initial violin theme, brutally cut short by a thud on the bass drum. In tones of desperation and despair, the soloist sings the final lines.

5:20–21

Why have you forgotten us forever, and forsaken us for so long?

Return us to You, Lord . . .

The prayer to return to God ushers in a coda for orchestra alone, based entirely on the pleading motive from the first movement announced first by solo string quartet before being taken up by the larger string section. This consoling idea brings the work to a close on a soft final chord whose mild dissonance is both hopeful and uncertain.

Throughout this movement you might notice just how sensitively Bernstein has set the text. Every word is clearly audible. The orchestra never covers the voice, even at the big climaxes, and the vocal line itself is impressively powerful: the proclamation of a prophet of God, only occasionally relaxing into a more lyrical mode. It's a really beautiful setting. More significantly, and perhaps because it was actually composed first, it resolves the tension created in the symphony's first two parts—if not necessarily happily—then with a rightness, an inevitability, that all good symphonic writing aspires to achieve.

In this last respect it's worth quoting Bernstein's own remarks during sessions for his last recording of the work (with the Israel Philharmonic and mezzo-soprano Christa Ludwig in 1977): "Although everything I write seems to have literary or dramatic underpinning, it is, after all, *music* that I am writing. Whatever happens in the music happens because of what the music does, not because of the words or extramusical ideas." Hopefully you have been able to hear the truth of this observation for yourself as it concerns the "Jeremiah" Symphony.

# Symphony No. 2 ("The Age of Anxiety") (1949, rev. 1965)

*Scoring: solo piano, piccolo, 2 flutes, 2 oboes, English horn, two clarinets, bass clarinet, 2 bassoons, contrabassoon, 4 horns, 3 trumpets, 3 trombones, tuba, snare drum, tenor drum, bass drum, cymbals, triangle, glockenspiel, xylophone, temple blocks, trap set (suspended cymbal with pedal bass drum), timpani, 2 harps, celesta, pianino (upright piano in the orchestra), and strings*

Like his First Symphony, Bernstein's Second is very much a wartime work, just as is the 1946 W. H. Auden poem that inspired it. Auden subtitled "The Age of Anxiety," which runs to some ninety pages in the Modern Library edition of his collected poetry, "A Baroque Eclogue," for whatever that's worth. An *eclogue* is usually defined as a pastoral poem of classical Greek origin, often taking the form of a dialogue between shepherds. In other words, the speakers are common folk, the theory being that nothing is (or was) as common as a shepherd. Auden has updated and translated the usual, rural setting to a bar on Manhattan's Third Avenue during the Second World War. Along with several other members of Britain's artistic elite (composer Benjamin Britten and his partner, tenor Peter Pears, being the most noteworthy musical examples), Auden had decamped to the United States at the outbreak of hostilities, arriving in 1939 and taking American citizenship in 1946—actions for which his reputation in the United Kingdom suffered.

For much of his life, Auden's work was intimately associated with music and musicians. His poetry provided the text of Britten's song cycle *Our Hunting Fathers*, and with lover Chester Kallman he coauthored the libretto of Stravinsky's neoclassical masterpiece *The Rake's Progress*. Nevertheless, it would not be an exaggeration to claim that the finest musical work that Auden inspired remains Bernstein's Second Symphony. Indeed, it has sometimes been hailed as finer (of its type) than the original, particularly by literary critics who do not number "The Age of Anxiety" among Auden's stronger efforts, though obviously direct comparison is pretty much impossible, if not pointless.

Auden's poem describes four characters, one woman (Rosetta) and three men (Quant, Emble, and Malin), whose curious names might be expected of a poet whose own first name was Wystan. They meet in the aforementioned bar, discuss the meaning of life, get drunk, have a sort of collective out-of-body experience, feel miserable, then take a cab to Rosetta's place to party. Quant and Malin eventually leave, exhausted. Emble stays behind and he and Rosetta almost fool around, but he passes out first—to her mixture of disappointment and relief—and life goes on the next day filled with a sort of numb, uncomprehending hopefulness (inasmuch as we can tell). Is all of this reflected in Bernstein's symphony? Well, yes and no.

As you can see, "The Age of Anxiety" tells the story of four characters, but there is a fifth as well, a narrator who sets the scene and comments on their thoughts and actions. The narrator summarizes and concludes the evening's activities in this way: "Facing another long day of servitude to wilful authority and blind accident, creation lay in pain and earnest, once more reprieved from self-destruction, its adoption, as usual, postponed."* This observation seems a far cry from the massive hopefulness of Bernstein's musical apotheosis, which he describes in his preface to the score as an affirmation of faith. In 1949, Bernstein was eager to highlight the music's close relationship to the detailed narrative structure of the poem, but in 1965, after revising the work to give the piano soloist a greater role in the last movement, "Epilogue," this was less of a concern.

The fact of the matter is that, ultimately, musical values override slavish adherence to any scheme of literal description in tones, as they must in any successful symphonic work. We can see this most obviously simply by noting that Auden includes four protagonists, whereas Bernstein requires only one (the piano soloist). Indeed, one of the criticisms leveled against "The Age of Anxiety" as literature has been that Auden's four modern-day "shepherds" seem to have little independent existence as individuals, a failing (if that's what it is) that Bernstein's musical treatment neatly avoids. This means, first, that there is no particular need for listeners to read Auden's poem to gain special understanding of the symphony's expressive message, and second, whichever aspects of the original that Bernstein has adapted most tellingly are those that naturally suggest musical treatment in the first place.

For example, consider Auden's description of his poem as "A Baroque Eclogue" in which the speakers, instead of being shepherds, become four "working-class Joes" getting drunk in a Manhattan bar. Bernstein was the ideal composer to capture this aspect of the poem in musical terms, effortlessly integrating popular music and jazz idioms into the structure and conventions of the classical symphony. Indeed, we could argue that music achieves this modernizing of a classical form far more easily than does a literary work, as Auden asks the reader to have at least some familiarity with his models; and outside of university classes in ancient Greek and Roman poetry, this is extremely unlikely. In music, on the other hand, not only will a listener to Bernstein's symphony

---

* W. H. Auden, *Collected Poems*, ed. Edward Mendelson (New York: Modern Library, 2007), 533.

have experience of other great works in the form, the internal contrast within the work between its thematic material's various idioms essentially speaks for itself.

Similarly, Auden's somewhat precious reference to his poem as "baroque" suggests an elaboration of language markedly at odds with the ordinariness of the scenario and the nominal characters. There's no question that this tension was part of Auden's plan, and inherent in the very idea of average people thinking and speaking in poetry, but again, it's a concept that music, particularly wordless music, achieves more easily, and perhaps more digestibly. Bernstein's "baroque" qualities find realization at many levels: in the elaborately ornamental solo piano writing; in the use of certain traditional musical forms (such as the variations in the symphony's first part); and most of all, in his choice of form for the work as a whole: that known historically as a *sinfonia concertante*.

Concertante symphonies are basically hybrid works that combine the well-defined solos (often for multiple instruments) of a concerto with the close thematic development and large-scale, multimovement forms of the symphony. The most famous examples in the modern repertoire are Mozart's Sinfonia Concertante for Violin, Viola, and Orchestra; Haydn's so-called Symphony No. 105 for oboe, bassoon, violin, cello, and orchestra; and Berlioz's "Harold in Italy" Symphony for solo viola and orchestra. However, the most famous composer of concertante symphonies was Johann Christian Bach (1735–1782), son of Johann Sebastian, known as the "English Bach." He flourished in the rococo period, roughly 1750–80, between the late baroque represented by his father and Handel, and the mature classical era of Haydn, Mozart, and Beethoven (he befriended and influenced the young Mozart).

So in choosing the form of the concertante symphony for "The Age of Anxiety," Bernstein captures at a stroke the baroque quality of Auden's original, but in purely musical terms that once again pose no particular barriers to comprehension—something that certainly cannot be said of the poem's complex and richly allusive language. Both works remain very much of their own time and place: reflections on the war and on the difficulty of forming and sustaining meaningful personal relationships in an urbanized, post-Holocaust, postatomic age. What Bernstein's symphony does particularly well is to universalize these ideas in a way that, as with all classics, frees them from the specific circumstances of their initial inspiration and date of composition, rendering them timelessly relevant.

## GUIDE TO LISTENING

One of the niftiest aspects of Auden's original poem is its presentation in a form that can only be called *musical*. It consists of a prologue followed by two sections clearly suggestive of variations on a theme ("The Seven Ages" and "The Seven Stages"), a dirge (funeral march), a masque (party music, or scherzo), and an epilogue that recalls the themes of the prologue. Bernstein had no problem organizing this material into a perfectly balanced, two-part symphony that plays for about half an hour, with each part containing three sections:

Part One:
a. Prologue
b. "The Seven Ages" (variations I–VII)
c. "The Seven Stages" (variations VIII–XIV)

Part Two:
a. "The Dirge"
b. "The Masque"
c. Epilogue

### Part I
#### Prologue

The Prologue presents the symphony's principal theme as a duet for two clarinets, lonely and wistful, and also very soft. Bernstein asks that they play "echo tone"; that is, with a "white" sound without any vibrato until nearly the end of their duet, when for a moment they adopt a natural, expressive timbre before returning to the opening theme, triple *piano*. If you remember the first phrase, eight notes long, of the clarinet theme, you will have in mind all you need to follow the ensuing variations, and much later music besides. The Prologue ends with the quiet entrance of the low harp, timpani, cellos *molto vibrato,* and a descending scale on the first flute, followed by a brief recollection of the clarinet theme from the second flute. The descending scale will also play an important part in the music to come.

### "The Seven Ages"

In this section, as Bernstein tells us in the preface to the score, "The life of man is reviewed from the four personal points of view." More important, "This is a series of variations which differ from conventional variations in that they do not vary any one common theme. Each variation seizes upon some feature of the preceding one and develops it, introducing, in the course of the development, some counter-feature upon which the next variation seizes."

Variation I: A solo piano, marked "pure and singing," plays a more hopeful version of the opening clarinet theme. The first phrase is inverted (that is, played upside down), before returning to its more familiar shape. Toward the end, the descending scale first played by the flute in the Prologue reappears as a harp solo, increasing in speed and volume. This scale becomes the principal subject of:

Variation II: Far longer and more elaborate than the preceding variation, the piano once again leads, but the entire orchestra (except the heavy brass) eventually participates in rich cascades of rising and falling scales. "Romantically," Bernstein tells the soloist, and *molto rubato* (that is, with a very free tempo). Toward the end, after the piano reaches a climax, a new idea appears briefly, followed by the now-familiar descending scales in the flute and harp. This new motive is developed in the next variation.

Variation III: The piano does not play. Instead, the violins sing out a warm tune over a plodding, pizzicato (plucked) bass line. This is immediately repeated by the horns, and then by a solo violin playing the same theme inverted (notice the similarity of procedure, but not the actual melody, with the pianist's handling of the opening theme in Variation I). When the full violin section reenters, Bernstein gives it a tiny, four-note motive that the piano grabs in a quicker tempo and turns into:

Variation IV: Beginning lightly and gracefully, with a hint of sparkle from the glockenspiel, the piano once again takes center stage. This variation has a definite ABA shape, and it is the B section's loud violin theme in long notes, conveniently speeded up at the very end of the variation in the piano and xylophone, that serves as the main idea of:

Variation V: Marked "agitated" and led off by a clarinet in its lowest register, this is an angular, gawky march very much in the spirit of Shostakovich, a composer Bernstein admired and performed frequently. The piano takes over the theme from the clarinet very quickly, accompanied by the dry sounds of bass drum (with a snare drumstick), snare drum (with brushes), and *col legno* strings (played with the wooden back of the bow to make a distinct, clicking sound). The full orchestra joins in, and the march becomes increasingly raucous and grotesque, breaking off suddenly and leaving the solo flute hanging for three bars with the motive of the next variation.

Variation VI: Bernstein introduces a brief cadenza for the piano alone, reflective and, as he marks it, "hesitant." As if by accident, the soloist wanders into the clarinet theme of the Prologue by way of introducing:

Variation VII: Effectively a recapitulation of the Prologue, all of the familiar material returns. Oboe and English horn play a variation of the initial clarinet duet, before those instruments return briefly with their original version. The flute's descending scale, greatly extended, now goes to the piano soloist, with the main theme superimposed on top along the way. Soft chords in the flutes and clarinets bring this section to a tranquil close. Notice how considerate Bernstein has been to his listeners, offering a review of the main thematic material before moving on the work's next phase. There is no conflict here, as there so often is in twentieth-century music, between formal or technical virtuosity, and comprehensibility.

"The Seven Stages"

By now our four protagonists are thoroughly drunk and ready for their next experience. Bernstein describes it thusly: "The variation form continues for another set of seven, in which the characters go on an inner and highly symbolic journey according to a geographical plan leading back to a point of comfort and security. The four try every means, going singly and in pairs, exchanging partners, and always missing the objective. When they awaken from this dream-odyssey, they are closely united through a common experience (and through alcohol), and begin to function as one organism. This set of variations begins to show activity and drive and leads to a hectic, though indecisive, close."

If the above looks confusing, try reading the poem! Happily, the music couldn't be clearer, and it reveals very interestingly the primacy of the musical process over mere illustrative writing. Although this section nominally contains the next seven variations, the fact is that Nos. XI–XIV (that is, that last four of them) comprise a single large, continuous fugue. The form of variations and fugue is one of the oldest in Classical music, another factor making this particular eclogue "baroque," but the essential point is that although Bernstein can say legitimately that he's following the structure of poem in offering two separate groups of seven variations, what the listener actually experiences in real time is a single span containing ten variations plus a concluding fugue—in other words, a far more satisfying discourse on purely musical grounds.

Variation VIII: In character, this variation resembles Variation III in that it features a full-toned violin theme over a plodding bass, but emotionally it's much gloomier. Musically it's based on the descending scale that closed the previous section, with its chromatic intervals (that is, moving in half-steps). The entrance of the piano, in a quicker rhythm, makes this relationship particularly evident, and the piano's theme generates the next variation, which is:

Variation IX: An ebullient but rhythmically awkward waltz featuring the violins, piano solo, and some sardonic interjections from the trumpets and xylophone. Eventually abandoning any pretense of trying to be an actual waltz, the variation stomps to a close with a series of violent exchanges between the soloist on the one hand, and the united woodwinds, brass, and timpani on the other. These outbursts generate:

Variation X: A skittish piano solo leads off, followed by the woodwinds, violins, horns, third trombone, and finally the xylophone. You might call this a "variation by reduction," because the music all boils down to a rhythmic leaping figure that becomes in the next variation:

Variation XI: The subject of a singularly grotesque little fugue, with the theme broken up by pauses of irregular length. The melodic voices enter in the following order: piano right hand, piano left hand, upper strings, high woodwinds, woodwinds plus xylophone, and solo trumpet (with thudding timpani strokes). As you may have noticed, the music is now becoming more continuous, and the next variations follow on one another without a break, in basically the same quick tempo.

Variation XII: The piano continues with a rhythmically smoothed-out development of the fugue theme. Pizzicato strings and flutes provide just a couple of perky interjections to mark the ends of the solo's phrases. In technical jargon, and if we consider the preceding and following variations to be part of the same larger fugue, this tiny variation counts as an "episode," or a moment of contrast.

Variation XIII: Over the quick piano tune of the previous variation, the low brass now enter with an augmented version of the same theme (that is, it's played in longer note values). It builds up in what's called a *stretto*: rapidly overlapping entries, working their way initially through the brass section. Trumpet and glockenspiel take up the tune frantically, in double time, followed by the lower strings, trombones, and tuba. The rest of the orchestra quickly gets involved leading to a snare drumroll, a cymbal crash, and a furious climax that propels the music into:

Variation XIV: We have now reached the coda to the fugue, and to the entire first half of the work. The soloist bangs out the main theme of the previous variation triple *forte* in vicious eighth notes, building rapidly to a shattering climax for the full orchestra that comes suddenly to a halt with a crash on the cymbals and a thud on the bass drum.

## Part II
### "The Dirge"

"'The Dirge'," Bernstein notes, "is sung by the four as they sit in a cab en route to the girl's apartment for a nightcap. They mourn the loss of the 'colossal Dad,' the great leader who can always give the right orders, find the right solution, shoulder the mass responsibility, and satisfy the universal need for a father-symbol. This section employs, in a harmonic way, a twelve-note row out of which the main theme evolves. There is a contrasting middle section of almost Brahmsian romanticism, in which can be felt the self-indulgent, or negative aspect of this strangely pompous lamentation."

Bernstein's own description of this music is curious for several reasons. The twelve-note row that he mentions appears right at the beginning, as a softly dissonant chord built up by the piano soloist. That aside, the music is as tonal as anything else in the symphony, and Bernstein's decision to point out this aspect of the music says more about what was expected of a contemporary composer, circa 1949, than it does about the movement's own very special expressive qualities. You may well feel, as I do, that the "Brahmsian romanticism" of the middle section isn't "negative" or "self-indulgent" at all—merely lovely, and not particularly "Brahmsian." Bernstein obviously is writing under the influence of the poem, but the music, taken on its own, will speak differently to each listener.

The first thing you might notice from a purely musical point of view is that the opening of "The Dirge" is scored entirely for piano, winds, and percussion, perhaps in homage to a very old tradition of symphonic funeral music (as in Berlioz's *Grande symphonie funèbre et triomphale*). The result is an unforgettable, hard, gleaming sonority. Second, although the variation portion of the work formally has ended, the musical material of these next two sections (that is, "The Dirge" and "The Masque") is even more clearly based on the opening theme of the Prologue than much of the previous Part One. This fact highlights just how well planned the symphony is formally speaking, and how intelligent Bernstein's decision really was to make the first part a series of "developing" variations, rather than a set of merely repetitious, ornamental elaborations of the same tune.

The virtue of his strategy becomes especially evident in considering the form of this movement a bit more closely. Using letters, the shape of "The Dirge" is ABACA(BC). Section A is the funeral march proper; B is a melody for the full string section decorated with twelve-note flourishes from the piano and juicy whacks on the tam-tam; whereas C, after a brief return of the initial march for the full orchestra, is that central "romantic" interlude for piano and (at first) strings, based quite audibly on the main theme of the Prologue. The march returns once more, just the bare rhythm (without the tune) in a brutal *fortissimo* for full orchestra, and the movement concludes with a transitional coda consisting of the string theme B, played by the violins *vibratissimo*, followed by C softly and "nostalgically" from the soloist. It is this tune, speeded up, that becomes the main idea of the next section.

## "The Masque"

Another updating of a classical form, "The Masque" consists of a scherzo (quick dance) and trio (middle section) that comes around twice, ABABA, a favorite device of Beethoven's (check out the scherzos in his Fourth, Sixth, and Seventh symphonies). Its scoring is wonderful: just piano, harps, celesta, and percussion. The "trio" section is a classic Bernstein pop tune, rounded off by the tick-tock of the two temple blocks. Note also Bernstein's delicious use of the celesta as an adjunct to the sonority of the piano. In length "The Masque" usually runs about five minutes, just a minute or so less than "The Dirge," and its very quick speed and hyper-jazzy idiom make it a real virtuoso showpiece for the pianist. It's also, for many listeners, the most purely entertaining and fun part of the whole symphony despite the fact that it theoretically represents a sadly desperate determination to have a good time.

Bernstein wrote, "The party ends in anticlimax and the dispersal of the actors; in the music the piano-protagonist is traumatized by the intervention of the orchestra for four bars of hectic jazz. When the orchestra stops, as abruptly as it began, a pianino [upright piano] in the orchestra is continuing the "Masque," repetitiously and with waning energy, as the Epilogue begins. Thus a kind of separation of the self from the guilt of escapist living has been effected, and the protagonist is free again to examine what is left beneath the emptiness." Or at least, that is what Bernstein initially planned, but he very soon realized that this sort of verbal specificity really lies beyond the scope of purely instrumental music to express, and that the work, however inspired by Auden it may have been initially, had its own story to tell.

## Epilogue

Initially, the "trauma" of "The Masque" caused the pianist to remain silent for the entire Epilogue until the penultimate bar. Bernstein understood, however, that having the solo sit there for the final six or seven minutes doing nothing made no musical sense. As he put it: "In the years that have past since 1949, I have reevaluated my attempt to mirror Auden's literary images in so literal a way." And so he revised the finale to include the soloist, even to the point of writing a cadenza (a sort of summing-up based on the themes of the symphony), just as in many a traditional piano concerto. This, perhaps, is even more faithful to the spirit of Auden's "Baroque Eclogue" than Bernstein's initial, more literal conception, and it not incidentally makes the hopeful concluding apotheosis even more convincing because of the additional opportunity both for contrast and recapitulation of previously heard material.

Thus, the Epilogue starts out with the woodwinds uttering a motive evocative of "something pure," as Bernstein put it. This alternates with reminiscences of the Prologue's opening theme from the soloist. The dialogue continues, working up to a climax in the orchestra, broken off suddenly for the cadenza—a final meditation on the expressive distance traveled, accompanied by triple-*piano* memories of "The Masque," played by the pianino. Unlike the traditional concerto cadenza, which usually ends in a bravura flourish and trill, this one goes quietly to sleep with a last whispered reference to the Prologue. Then the full orchestra enters "with serenity," the strings *molto vibrato*, building inexorably to a grand climax with bells, tam-tam, and finally the piano soloist, sounding notes of joyous affirmation.

Bernstein recorded this symphony three times, first in 1950 for Sony Classical (then Columbia) with Lukas Foss as the brilliant piano soloist, and that version naturally preserves the Epilogue's original version. You can hear it for yourself if you're curious. More important, the history of this symphony, arguably Bernstein's finest, shows him moving from a young composer's anxiety to do justice to the original source of his inspiration to a more mature confidence in his craft, and in the ability of the music to stand on its own away from its literary model. This must have been fortified by the knowledge that, by 1965, Bernstein's symphony was well on its way to becoming better known and certainly more popular than Auden's poem ever will be, a situation that the passing of another half century has only confirmed.

## Symphony No. 3 ("Kaddish") (1963)

*Scoring: speaker, soprano solo, mixed chorus, boys' choir, piccolo, 4 flutes, alto flute, 2 oboes, English horn, alto saxophone, E-flat clarinet, 2 clarinets, bass clarinet, 2 bassoons, contrabassoon, 4 horns, trumpet in D, 3 trumpets, 3 trombones, tuba, vibraphone, xylophone, glockenspiel, snare drum, field drum, tenor drum, bass drum, Israeli hand drum, cymbals, finger cymbals, antique cymbals, tam-tam, 3 bongos, 3 temple blocks, woodblock, sandpaper blocks, rasp, whip, ratchet, triangle, maracas, claves, tambourine, chimes, harp, piano, celesta, and strings*

There's a certain irony to the fact that the "Kaddish" Symphony is Bernstein's most controversial large work, not because it's in any way difficult or obscure; rather, for just the opposite reason: What it wants to say is perfectly obvious because it just, well, comes out and says it. Literally. The work is basically a forty-minute-long discussion and argument between mankind, in the person of the speaker—whether male or female—and God, who musically remains a mysterious, silent presence. In the Second Symphony, Bernstein addressed the question of our ability to find meaningful relationships among ourselves. Here he takes the process to another level, trying to imagine a more healthy and productive relationship between man and his Creator. A tall order, perhaps, but sometimes it's the effort that's more important than achieving an unqualified success. As in Goethe's *Faust*, the "Kaddish" Symphony suggests the possibility of redemption through striving. It attempts to justify and sanctify the inevitability of constant struggle with our own imperfections (and, radical notion, God's too, since he made us that way in his own image).

This program, embodied in Bernstein's own spoken text, has been criticized from any number of perspectives: It's pretentious, hysterical, embarrassing, doctrinally offensive, self-indulgent, and basically just plain ridiculous. The music has also come in for its share of adverse comment. The atonal bits represent a lame attempt on Bernstein's part to sound "relevant" circa 1963, while the tonal parts are derivative and facile. In particular, the Big Tune that appears at the end of the scherzo sounds like the bastard child of Bach's "Jesu, Joy of Man's Desiring" and Copland's "Simple Gifts" from *Appalachian Spring*. And perhaps it is, but it's still one hell of a good tune, and snobbery aside the rest of the music is pretty fabulous too, even spectacular.

Indeed, "Kaddish" has only seemed to grow more impressive over time, and the work has been staging something of a comeback in recent years, with an increasing number of performances and several new recordings. Bernstein's daughter tried to deal with the problem (if such it is) of the spoken dialogue by rewriting it—a sincere but misconceived effort that only served to prove pretty definitively that Bernstein's original thoughts were much better. So there's no point in pretending that the piece doesn't really say what Bernstein so clearly intended it to say. Either you like it (or at least accept it) or you don't. It's a question of taste, plain and simple.

However, a musical issue that "Kaddish" raises is worth discussing in a bit more depth. Like the Second Symphony and *Serenade*, both of which represent modern, creative reinterpretations of older genres (the concertante symphony in the case of the former, the concerto in the latter), the Third Symphony does something similar. Here the genre in question is the melodrama, which simply means a spoken scene or drama accompanied by music throughout. Imagine a film with a virtually continuous soundtrack beneath, and you get the idea. Most of Bernstein's musicals include bits of melodrama, as do many operas of all periods. The most famous modern example of a melodrama in the orchestral repertoire is probably Copland's *A Lincoln Portrait*. However, another outstanding instance occurs in the prison scene in the second act of Beethoven's *Fidelio*.

The genre became wildly popular in the second half of the eighteenth century. Outstanding works were composed from the 1770s on, starting with Georg Benda's *Ariadne auf Naxos*, and followed by important examples from Mozart's Mannheim colleague Christian Cannabich, and also Georg Vogler, famous today as the teacher of Carl Maria von Weber and Giacomo Meyerbeer. Many of these composers, particularly the large and musical Benda family (there are still members of it around today), came from the Czech lands, and it was there that the genre really took off. Nineteenth-century Czech composer Zdeněk Fibich brought the melodrama to its apex when he composed, between 1889 and 1891, *Hippodamia*, a full-blown Wagnerian trilogy, with each installment lasting a good couple of hours or more.

After that brief apotheosis, the melodrama practically disappeared as an independent musical or theatrical genre, replaced by the achievements of the nascent film industry. Just how much of this history Bernstein was aware of (probably a lot) or cared about remains an open question. What matters is that the "Kaddish" Symphony revives this moribund tradition in a most creative and colorful way. Bernstein conceived the part of the speaker for his wife, the actress Felicia Montealegre, and she recorded it with him, bringing an unforgettable histrionic intensity and conviction to words that might otherwise fall flat. When she shrieks, "Tin God! Your bargain is tin! It crumples in my hand," your first instinct is to wait for lightening to strike, and when it doesn't, to call an ambulance.

That said, the presence of so much talk can make "Kaddish" a tough nut to swallow for those who find speech combined with music simply irritating, especially when the music promises to be really interesting and worth hearing all by itself. I have to confess to being one of those people, feeling the music of "Kaddish" to be enthralling but the spoken text annoying, at least initially—not so much because of what it says, but merely because it exists in the first place. Plenty of people are more than happy to yell at me; I don't want a symphony to do it. However, if my own personal experience is any help, I have found that with time any objections largely have vanished. Familiarity has led to enjoyment of Bernstein's conception as a totality, and to admiration for its expressive directness and formal concision.

So much for the presence of the spoken text. Now we move on to the sung part. The Kaddish is the traditional Jewish prayer of mourning, although it exists in several versions which are recited at different times during worship, and for different purposes. It is one of the best known of all parts of the Hebrew liturgy. Interestingly, the prayer makes no mention of death; rather, it praises God and life, and asks for peace. Here is the complete text of the version recited by the bereaved after the passing of a loved one:

> Mourner's Kaddish
>
> Glorified and sanctified be the great name of God throughout the world, which He made as He willed. May He establish His kingdom in your lifetime and during your days, and within the lifetime of the whole House of Israel, speedily and soon; and let us say, Amen.
>
> May His great name be blessed forever and for all eternity.
>
> Blessed and praised, glorified and exalted, extolled and hon-ored, adored and acclaimed be the name of the Holy One, blessed be He, beyond all the blessings and hymns, praises and songs of adoration that have ever been spoken; and let us say, Amen.
>
> May there be abundant peace from heaven, and life for us and for all Israel; and let us say, Amen.
>
> May he who creates peace in the heavens grant peace to us and to all Israel; and let us say, Amen.

## GUIDE TO LISTENING

The "plot" of the symphony, such as it is, closely resembles that of *Mass*, the work closest to "Kaddish" conceptually in Bernstein's output. Both works examine the crisis of faith that Bernstein saw as one of the principal malaises of twentieth-century life, and both organize the exploration of this crisis around performance of particular liturgy. The symphony is organized in three parts that play continuously, but it also encompasses the traditional four symphonic movements:

*Part 1:*
a. Introduction
b. [first movement] Allegro (Kaddish 1)

*Part 2:*
a. Introduction ("Din Torah")
b. [second movement] Andante con tenerezza (Kaddish II)

*Part 3:*
a. [third movement] Scherzo
b. [fourth movement] Finale (Kaddish III)

In both Parts I and II, the introduction contains most of the melodrama and the two Kaddish settings form the main, purely musical body of the movement. In the scherzo and finale, melodrama and singing alternate. The first part of Kaddish III is sung by the boys' choir at the end of the scherzo, leaving the remainder to close the finale. Because the symphony has either a spoken or a sung text basically throughout, the best way to listen is to follow the words as they are spoken. Don't worry about keeping up with the Hebrew text of the Kaddish. You know what it means, so just listen and enjoy the music. There's also no need to go into formal details at length. We can take the work's structural integrity for granted. Here is a brief synopsis of each major section.

## Part I

### Introduction

Against a background of soft humming from the chorus, the speaker announces her desire to say Kaddish for herself (and by implication all mankind) before it's too late. She* worries that time is running out, and that there maybe be no one to say the prayer in her memory once she

---

* For simplicity's sake I will continue to refer to the speaker as "she," in keeping with Bernstein's original conception for the role.

is gone. A quick word of explanation on this particular point: Judaism, in all but its most mystical or orthodox forms, lacks a clear doctrinal foundation for belief in an afterlife. Accordingly, it places a very strong emphasis on keeping the memories of the dead alive through prayer and other rituals of remembrance (such as the naming of children). It's also worth mentioning, relative to Bernstein's own concerns, that 1963 was the height of the cold war, and the threat of nuclear annihilation was very much on people's minds. Bernstein's text refers to this specifically later on.

In addition to the choral humming, at strategic points during this opening speech the orchestra interjects an ominous commentary in abrupt, jerky rhythms. This motive is one of Bernstein's melodic archetypes, often used in his music expressing anguish, suffering, or lamentation. Something very similar reappears in *Mass*, both in the setting of the "De profundis" ("From the depths I cried to you, Lord"), and as the main theme of the first of the *Three Meditations* that Bernstein later arranged for cello and orchestra. It will become the music of "*Yitgadal v'yitkaddash*," the first words of the Kaddish. With its rhythm and phrasing smoothed out, this motive also generates the Big Tune representing faith that emerges at the end of the Scherzo.

## Kaddish I

An angry, violent dance for the full choir, featuring much foot stomping and hand clapping in addition to other percussive effects, erupts without warning. The basic idiom is atonal, but nonetheless melodic, and so fierce is the music's energy and rhythmic drive that the effect is very exhilarating. As the Kaddish draws to a close, the speaker picks up on the choral shouts of "Amen," and repeats in English the last line of the prayer, the plea for peace. Taken up by the choir, this closes the first part in a state of high agitation and extreme aggression.

## Part II

### Introduction

A Din Torah is a Jewish court proceeding, a "judgment by law." Here it is God himself who is on trial. The speaker accuses God of breaking his covenant with man, and of basically letting the world go to hell. This is the part of the symphony that, understandably, aroused the most strenuous objections from defenders of traditional religious thinking (as if God needs them for protection). Even so, anyone who knows the Old Testament will understand that disputations and negotiations with God are very much part and parcel of the Jewish tradition. The speaker's text is accompanied mostly by percussion, a very threatening and effective sonority. At the climax of this section, the orchestra breaks in with a lengthy, anguished interlude interspersed by choral cries of "Amen," and ending with an eight-part choral cadenza in which "Amen" is sung in just about every conceivable rhythm and tempo—a modern Tower of Babel moment. This fades into silence.

## Kaddish II

The speaker apologizes for causing God such anguish and promises relief from suffering in sleep and dreams. The solo soprano and women's choir turn this second Kaddish into a lullaby having the simple form ABA, with B being a quicker contrasting section. The music is some of the most ravishingly lovely that Bernstein ever wrote, all the more so coming after the musical and verbal expression of so much anger, frustration, and violence.

## Part III

### Scherzo

This movement has two halves. God is asleep, and mankind is controlling his dream. The speaker takes God on an imaginary journey to the biblical heaven, revealing it to be a sterile place inhabited by people who are empty shells. They have nothing to strive for and no purpose in life. The music—mostly soft, very swift and light—admirably captures the aimless mechanical activity of this purported paradise. It also serves as a kind of gigantic development section involving most of the symphony's principle material, but it's impossible to pay attention to that and note what the speaker is saying at the same time, nor does it matter particularly. The idea is to create a delicate tapestry of sound against which the speaker can make her points.

In the movement's second half, God and speaker return to earth, and the speaker reminds God of his original promise—symbolized by the rainbow—and of the ancient time when miracles were still possible, and life seemed full of new possibilities. At this point, Bernstein introduces the Big Tune (based, as previously noted, on the initial Kaddish theme from the beginning of the symphony), and the speaker calls on God to believe in mankind once again—to renew his faith in his greatest creation. As the tune rises through the orchestra, the boys' choir begins Kaddish III. The possibility of a new covenant between God and man brings the scherzo to a hopeful close.

## Finale

Recalling the music of the "Din Torah," the finale begins with a harsh return to reality. After a brief introduction, the Big Tune appears quietly on the strings, and the speaker suggests the possibility a new, more mature relationship between God and man. Both need each other, and each creates and sustains the other in a sort of spiritual symbiosis. For all its imperfections, mankind still deserves God's love and faith. The remainder of Kaddish III brings all of the vocal forces together for first time, and continues developing the dance rhythms of the first part. The energy is the same, but the harmonies are now clearly tonal; the emotion, one of joy. At the last climax, the Big Tune explodes through the orchestra in a celebratory frenzy, and with jubilant cries of "Amen" the music rushes to a close.

In his first recording of the symphony for Columbia (now Sony Classical), the ending is a touch different: Bernstein decided to cut two striking choral glissandos to move straight through to the final crescendo—probably a good idea. He also eliminated some of the spoken text ("too much talking," he said), making the flow of music more continuous. Even with these changes, the last word on this ambitious symphony has yet to be written. It may be that Bernstein's proprietary ownership prevented others from risking new interpretations and giving it the kind of thoughtful attention it surely repays. Now that he is gone, and the music has to stand on its own, I wouldn't be a bit surprised to find that it does just that, and very successfully, too.

# *Serenade* after Plato's *Symposium* (1954)

*Scoring: solo violin, harp, timpani, snare drum, tenor drum, bass drum, cymbals, triangle, tambourine, glockenspiel, xylophone, Chinese blocks, chimes, and strings*

If a composer manages to write a great violin concerto, then the chances are he's a great composer generally. No genre, not even the piano concerto, features a larger number of truly lousy pieces. Part of the problem is that violinists are a notoriously snippy breed, always ready to complain, whatever the masterpiece of the orchestral repertoire on their music stand, that its author really didn't understand how to write correctly for the violin. The truth is that great orchestral music and great solo violin music are not only hard to find in the same work, they are to some extent incompatible. The violin is a melody instrument, and so to hold its own against anything that can produce a full mass of harmony (like a piano, never mind the orchestra), it has to indulge in what can come to sound like an endless babble of mindless figuration.

Of course, the violin is unsurpassed at spinning out long, lyrical cantabile (songlike) tunes and the nineteenth century is full of beautiful slow movements, but these only constitute one third of a typical concerto. The rest of the time, especially in quicker music, either a dysfunctional approach to form (a problem endemic to romantic concertos generally), a horror of giving the full ensemble anything that risks upstaging the solo, or some combination of these two problems, makes listening a chore. Think of a scenario involving a desperately vain coloratura soprano pretending that the faster and louder she sings without taking a breath, the less you'll notice that there's a tenor, a chorus, and an entire orchestra participating as well, hoping to be given something useful to do.

As a result of this lamentable state of affairs, in the nineteenth century the "best" violin concertos, meaning the most idiomatic from the player's point of view, were written by a slew of second-rate composer/performers that no one cares about today: names such as Spohr, Vieuxtemps, Wieniawski, and Rode, among many others. Yet you can count on the fingers of one hand the most important works in the genre by the best composers, many of whom happened to be pianists by training: Beethoven, Mendelssohn, Tchaikovsky, and Brahms. With a little assistance from the other hand, you can include Bruch, Dvořák, Sibelius, and Elgar. Most of these men, even professional string players such as the last three just listed, wrote only a single violin concerto, a testament to how much effort it cost them. As the twentieth century wore on, however, the situation began to change.

There were several reasons for this, prime among them the rise of virtuoso violinists who were not also composers writing mainly to provide themselves with individual, proprietary concert repertoire. These artists needed music of quality. They were willing to work with composers in commissioning new works, and to learn to master their technical difficulties—even the occasional awkwardness. The result of this symbiotic relationship was a splendid modern repertoire of excellent violin concertos by composers as diverse as Szymanowski, Bartók, Walton, Britten, Shostakovich, Martinů, Berg, Hindemith, Prokofiev, Barber, and not least, Leonard Bernstein. All of these composers wrote pieces that have become (or deserve to become) repertory standards.

But despite the fact that there are more worthy twentieth-century violin concertos than we find in centuries past, they still remain comparatively rare, and precious whenever we find them. This is because even though the circumstances for their creation by the best composers may be more favorable now, violin concertos remain tremendously difficult undertakings. Setting aside the problem of a nonvirtuoso writing credibly for the instrument, the medium represents a veritable minefield when it comes to problems of balance and ensemble. For this reason most violin concertos, even modern ones, call for reduced orchestral forces. Indeed, you can often tell from the scoring alone if the composer likely knows what he is doing. Bernstein's decision to restrict himself to harp, strings, and percussion is thus a hopeful sign, one which the end result reveals as inspired.

Like the earlier Second Symphony, the *Serenade* takes a literary work as its inspiration, and you may well wonder (as with the symphony) what features of the original Bernstein has attempted to capture in the music. Happily, he has answered this question for us:

> There is no literal program for this *Serenade*, despite the fact that
> it resulted from a re-reading of Plato's charming dialogue, "The
> Symposium." The music, like the dialogue, is a series of related
> statements in praise of love, and generally follows the Platonic
> form through the succession of speakers at the banquet. The "relat-
> edness" of the movements does not depend on common thematic
> material, but rather on a system whereby each movement evolves
> out of elements in the preceding one.

If you have read the discussion of the Second Symphony, you may
notice the similarity in Bernstein's description of both works' compositional process (a series of evolving variations), as well as their relationship to their respective literary inspirations. In the case of the *Serenade*
we are particularly fortunate the Bernstein has disavowed pictorial
specificity, because charming, amusing, and entertaining though much
of *The Symposium* undoubtedly is, Plato's celebration of sexual love
between men and boys (or at all events much younger men) can't help
but make many modern readers queasy. This is particularly true in light
of Bernstein's own well-publicized proclivities, though I hasten to add
that there was never, ever, any suggestion of pedophilia in his relationships with younger men. It would be equally unjust (and shallow) to
equate love, as Bernstein celebrates it here, merely with sex, an activity
that music in any event can't express in strictly pictorial terms at all.

Still, I have no doubt that the raunchier specifics of Plato as they
relate to the *Serenade* likely will become someone's dissertation (if it
hasn't happened already). Anything is possible in academia. Far more
pertinent to us as listeners is the fact that the concerto is the perfect
medium to realize in music the idea of a dialogue between an individual speaker, in this case the solo violin, and a larger audience (the
orchestra). But of course this piece is more than just a concerto; it is
a concerto in the form of a serenade, a genre with a long and vener-
able history as a musical expression of love. Most descriptions of the
term define *serenade* as a sort of loosely organized symphony with an
extra dance movement or two, often incorporating concerto elements.
Mozart's largest orchestral serenades, for example, have multimovement
violin concertos embedded in them.

However, the origins of the form go back further still, to street music played by itinerant musicians, and in particular to troubadours and small instrumental ensembles hired by gentlemen suitors to stand beneath a young lady's balcony and enchant her with songs of love and longing. Many a budding composer, Haydn for example, supplemented their income by performing serenades, and of course the custom still exists today, however jaded our modern view of such things. It is this delightful tradition that Bernstein's music evokes, mostly joyously, wistfully, and touchingly, without any of the existential angst or "crisis of faith" issues found in the three symphonies.

Over time, though, the word *serenade* did change its grammatical classification from a verb ("let's go and serenade that hot babe over on Main Street") to a noun, in the process becoming a distinct musical genre. By the nineteenth century its form had more or less settled down to a work in five (or more) movements, the typical example being Dvořák's *Serenade for Strings*. Indeed, concert serenades, meant to be played indoors, often featured string orchestras to distinguish them from the wind ensembles more typical of music written to sound best in the open air, and Bernstein's piece partakes of this tradition as well. In a concert setting, the romantic qualities of the strings more than compensate (hopefully) for the absence of the street or alley, a warm summer evening by a moonlit balcony, and the much-anticipated appearance of the theoretical object of one's desire.

## GUIDE TO LISTENING

Although Bernstein never seemed to have any problem talking about his own music, his comments on the *Serenade*, just cited, are deceptive. It may be that, for whatever reason, he didn't want us to focus on the common thematic material that the movements share, but the fact is that there's quite a bit of direct quotation going on between them above and beyond the variation process in which the work's main ideas participate. This makes the music strikingly easy to follow, as well as very strongly unified. Indeed, as you will hear, it's basically fair to say that the entire work grows out of the initial theme played by the solo violin right at the start. So if you hear a stronger similarity between the *Serenade*'s various parts than Bernstein's own remarks suggest, you're on solid ground.

## First Movement: "Phaedrus: Pausanias" (Lento: Allegro marcato)
### (CD Track 13)

As you can see, Bernstein names each movement after the participants in the actual symposium, but this has no particular significance as it concerns the expressive point of the music. That said, the fact that this first movement lists two characters does mean that it has two parts: an introduction and an ensuing allegro. The relationship between the two is very interesting. You may be familiar with certain keyboard pieces (most famously by Bach in his *Well-Tempered Clavier*) that take the form of a prelude and fugue. In other words, an opening section having a freeform, improvised character is followed by a highly organized, "architectural" movement using more or less strict counterpoint. Bernstein does just the opposite: this movement starts with a fugue, followed by a prelude. This strategy accomplishes several expressive goals with notable brilliance.

First, moving from the more complex form to the more relaxed admirably suits the character of the serenade as a genre: music for enjoyment, where any suggestion of pathos never turns tragic for long, or overwhelms its predominantly cheerful character. Second, the subject of this particular symposium is love, and of all musical forms the fugue most closely imitates an actual discussion. Indeed, the main theme of a fugue is called its "subject," and despite the fact that Bernstein doesn't want to illustrate the actual speeches in Plato, what he can do in purely musical terms is propose a subject and have various other voices consider it and agree to carry the conversation further.

That is exactly what this introduction accomplishes. Technically it's not a fully worked out fugue, but rather a fugato, a contrapuntal passage that gives the impression of being a fugue but that is actually part of something larger that may not be terribly fuguelike at all. Plato's subject being love, we can assume that the opening theme represents it too. Surely it's no coincidence that theme's initial motive of eight notes, played by the solo violin, ends with a three-note rising figure that Bernstein would borrow a few years later as the motive representing Maria in *West Side Story*.

This principle melody is remarkable both harmonically (bittersweet, wistful) and rhythmically. Its exceptional fluidity stems from the fact that its eight bars contain seven changes of meter: 7/8, 3/4, 5/8, 3/8, 3/4 (two bars), 5/8, and 3/8. In short, it serves as the perfect subject for future development, offering all kinds of opportunities for the sort of variation process that Bernstein plans to use. Another advantage to the fugato opening is that you get to hear the theme played three times, in a steady crescendo: first by the solo violin, then muted first violins, and muted violas. When the full string section enters it's only to build up a climax that, assisted by the suspended cymbals and a solid thwack on the timpani, initiates the allegro (at 2:56).

Bernstein describes the movement's quick second half as a "classical sonata-allegro," and so it is, but of a particular type very much in keeping with the spirit of the work. Most sonata form movements have three sections: an exposition presenting two contrasting themes (or groups of themes), a development section, and a recapitulation that restates all of the initial ideas in the movement's home key. Some, however, leave out the development section, as Bernstein does here. This usually happens in slow movements, because in music *slow* means "long." When a composer adopts this form for an allegro, it often means that the movement will be brief and, lacking a development section, lighter in character than usual. Famous examples include Mozart's overture to *The Marriage of Figaro*, and Bernstein's own most popular concert piece, the *Candide* Overture.

So this allegro truly is the prelude that follows the fugue, an introduction to the remainder of the *Serenade*, and to the discussion of love still to come. The first theme is simply a speeded-up version of the fugue subject. It's played first by the orchestra, and then by the solo violin mostly in double-stops (two note chords) with earthy, rustic good cheer. Bright percussion sonorities, triangle, glockenspiel, snare drum, and cymbals enhance the effect dramatically. At 3:45, the second theme sails in with waltzlike grace (though it's not actually in triple time for very long). As you can hear, it's yet another transformation of the main theme—its second phrase—now a bit skittish, but mostly relaxed and casual. The solo plays it twice through and, joined by the rest of the orchestra, reaches a triumphant march with celebratory chimes adding emphasis, before the tempo suddenly increases and a brief transition leads directly back to the beginning (5:01).

In vintage classical fashion, the restatement of the initial material isn't entirely literal, but compressed. The natural outcome of the entire movement's having been based on a single tune means you really don't need to hear it presented again at such length. Accordingly the solo and the orchestra, in smartly patterned dialogue, swiftly move through the two main ideas, the second of which serves as the subject of a brief coda that brings the movement to a close in a mood of uninhibited high spirits. The entire piece lasts about six and a half minutes, but you'll probably agree that its compactness only serves to emphasize its musical energy and bigness of spirit.

## Second Movement: "Aristophanes" (Allegretto) (CD Track 14)

Bernstein scores this delicate but sophisticated little movement for just the soloist, strings, and harp with no percussion at all. His use of the harp is especially sensitive and restrained; it adds just the occasional touch of color to the accompaniment. Formally speaking the piece has a simple ABA shape, but some nifty things happen within those two sections. The main theme begins, as you can plainly hear, where the previous movement left off—that is, with a variant of the second subject of the initial allegro. Rising and falling three-note figures built into both the melody and its muted accompaniment may also suggest the "Maria" motive that opened the *Serenade*.

After a couple seconds of prelude on the cellos, the solo violin presents the gentle main theme, and then this entire first idea becomes the accompaniment to a new lyrical melody sung out by the soloist (0:24). After a brief, passionate outburst in double stops, the violin alights on a sustained high note, and the middle section begins (1:15). The mutes come off, and violas present a new tune treated as a miniature set of variations. Its actual melody is really less important than the rhythm, a fact the Bernstein makes clear in the first variation, which consists of little else (1:34). Pay particular attention to this idea, because a very similar stripped-down rhythmic idea will feature prominently in the finale.

The next variation is a spiky exchange between solo violin and upper strings, versus the violas and cellos (with tiny flecks of harp as well). The solo violin then takes up both the original viola theme (2:09) and its purely rhythmic variant, first vigorously, then dreamily. All of this paves the way for a return of the initial A section, varied, as always with Bernstein, and even more ethereal than before. Sounding high in the violin, in broken phrases, the lyrical countermelody softly brings the movement to its conclusion, but not without a last reminiscence of the central viola tune in the very last few bars.

As you can hear, there's a tremendous amount of sheer craft in this mysterious, emotionally ambivalent little movement. It has the sort of elusiveness that grows on you with repeated listening.

## Third Movement: "Eryximachus" (Presto) (CD Track 15)

This tiny scherzo, lasting less than ninety seconds in all, brings back the percussion, most notably the xylophone, often a good musical indication of clowning or sardonic humor. It begins with the three-note "Maria" figure, and then it's off to the races with the solo violin scampering about in fast sixteenth notes, immediately repeated "with violence" by the full string section plus snare drum. Although you hear a single melody, Bernstein very cleverly breaks up the tune between the first and second violins, which helps to keep the ensemble rhythm together far better than if everyone had been forced to play with identical precision, imitating a single soloist from first note to last. This first section, after just a couple of exchanges, ends as it began, with the "Maria" motive.

The middle section (0:23) is a fugato based on the same material, led off by the soloist, and followed by the first and second violins, the divided violas, and divided cellos. It breaks off rudely when the full orchestra comes storming back in with the principal theme (0:55). Note the "Maria" motive hammered out as a timpani solo, which formally marks the return of the opening dialog, only now it diminishes in volume as it proceeds. The violin plays it first *sul ponticello*, or on the bridge of the instrument, which gives the music a distinctly thin, metallic character. Then the full string section interrupts, no longer "with violence," but in a steady decrescendo. Despite a final attempt at loudness from the orchestra, the movement whispers to a close at high speed just as it began, the last word going to the "Maria" motive on percussion alone (timpani, snare drum, and xylophone).

As I'm sure you'll agree, there's nothing especially funny about describing humor—when a joke has to be explained it's no longer a joke. Happily though, the music's dry, cartoonish wackiness makes an immediate impression when listening. It has always reminded me of the kind of thing we heard as kids watching *Looney Tunes* (think of the "Roadrunner"), an image that strikes me as far more in keeping with the character of this movement than any possible identification with the physician Eryximachus's speech in the *Symposium*. On the other hand, if you do feel like reading Plato, what passed for medical science in those days is sure to evoke a smile—and a shudder.

## Fourth Movement: "Agathon" (Adagio) (CD Track 16)

No major work by Bernstein would be complete without at least one warm, lyrical, romantic melody, and that found here is one of his best. Considering the subject of the *Serenade* as a whole, this tune is also remarkably pure and sweet, serene but also yearning. There's no sweaty, Wagnerian "love-death" in this music. The lack of musical heavy breathing reminds us yet again that as a composer Bernstein often showed himself to be a musician of notable taste and restraint, a fact often obscured by his flamboyant public persona. Scored only for strings, harp, and timpani, this Adagio has the same form as the second movement and the preceding scherzo: ABA, but once again Bernstein exploits it quite differently as regards the details.

Here, the A section is a single, gigantic melody for solo violin, the work's Big Tune. It's accompanied by the eight-note first phrase of the *Serenade*'s opening melody, though the last three notes, the "Maria" motive, don't appear just yet. Bernstein reserves his most literal quotation for the point, at 2:05, where the motive serves as a transition to the

B section, played by a solo violin in the orchestra. The middle episode has two parts, first, a passionate new melody on the violas (2:35), which may be a bit difficult to hear clearly because it's buried in the surrounding texture. The first violins take it up immediately, however, and over a growing timpani roll the orchestra builds to a passionate climax spilling over into a cadenza for the soloist.

Like most cadenzas, this one acts as a free improvisation or rhapsody on the music heard previously. Beginning *appassionato*, the music gradually calms down until at 4:59, the Big Tune returns even more sweetly and delicately than previously, coming to rest on a high, vibratoless harmonic tone beneath which the orchestra quietly goes to sleep. The mood and scoring here recall the ending of one of Mahler's most tender (and sad) works, the *Kindertotenlieder* (Songs on the Death of Children), a piece that Bernstein conducted and recorded several times. The text at that point reads: "They rest peacefully, as if in their mother's house." Bernstein, for his part, calls Agathon's oration "the most moving speech of the dialog."

### Finale: "Socrates: Alcibiades" (Molto tenuto; Allegro molto vivace) (CD Track 17)

The finale, at about eleven minutes, is the longest movement in the *Serenade*. Long symphony and concerto finales often are bad or at all events boring things. In the true classical style of the late eighteenth and early nineteenth centuries, the most intricate and extended movement was usually placed first and the music relaxed both formally and expressively as it proceeded. So Bernstein was taking a risk in placing his biggest and most intricate movement in last place. However, the fact that the music up to this point has been so concise and concentrated means that a more extended conclusion might be just the ticket, and so it proves. The full orchestra participates here, as it has not since the first movement.

"Socrates" contains the most tragic music in the *Serenade*, and it's based on the saddest theme presented thus far: the melody of the previous movement's B section. This very substantial introduction takes up more than a third of the movement (it ends at 4:09) and has its own distinct form: a powerful exordium for the full string section backed by chimes and timpani, a thoughtful dialogue in canon (one part follows the other with the same music) between the solo violin and a solo cello in a different key, and then a calming, diaphanously scored return of the opening tune now played by the solo violin and very softly accompanied by the divided violas and cellos.

Bernstein suggests that because this introduction consists of a highly developed reprise of previous material, it hints at a hidden sonata form for the work as a whole, something that the elements of thematic recall and recapitulation in the rest of the movement will confirm. Like the first movement, this finale also offers two for the price of one: a slow introduction leading to a quicker allegro. So the overall shape of the *Serenade* has a particularly satisfying balance of movements, an "arch" form typical of the kind of structure usually associated with the music of Hungarian composer Bela Bartók (his Concerto for Orchestra offers a typical example). Here the arch takes the shape: slow/fast–slow–fast–slow–slow/fast.

The finale's quick half starts with a bang. This rambunctious romp has a form similar to that of the first movement: sonata without development, although in this case each of its two parts (technically the exposition and recapitulation) has the shape of a rondo, basically a verse-and-refrain sequence that looks like this: ABACA, and so on. The first episode (B) is a lyrical theme for the solo violin that once again recalls the *Serenade*'s opening theme (4:51). The second (C) starts at 5:17 and recalls the rhythmic variation in the middle section of the second movement. Bernstein makes hearing the music's division into distinctive parts easy by placing a prominent stroke on the chime just before each one. The second episode is quite extended, turning into a deliciously dirty jazz excursion at 5:55. In all of this music the solo has been alternating with the orchestra in a dashing exchange of characterful variations on the basic material.

Gentle taps on the xylophone (6:55) initiate the recapitulation, which follows a course very similar to the exposition. This time, however, it leads to a very extensive coda (9:27) in triple time that wraps up the piece in dazzling fashion. Starting with the solo violin, we get a brief recap of the C episode before the main theme of the first movement joins in (10:09), and the solo races off at top speed into the final page to a zany accompaniment of Chinese block and xylophone, capped at the last by a joyous clangor of bells.

Bernstein thought the *Serenade* to be perhaps his "most satisfying" piece of purely instrumental music, and it's very difficult not to agree. It has all the dash and soul that we expect in a major violin concerto, but its style and idiom are pure Bernstein.


## *Halil* (1981)

*Scoring: solo flute, harp, timpani, 4 snare drums, 4 tom-toms, bass drum, cymbals, whip, 4 wood blocks, 2 triangles, 2 gongs, tam-tam, glockenspiel, xylophone, vibraphone, chimes, alto flute, piccolo, and strings*

*Halil* is the Hebrew word for "flute": the *H* is a guttural sound without an equivalent in English, the same as in the word Hanukkah, sometimes also spelled Chanukah. The score not very helpfully puts a little dot under the *h*, as if anyone knows what that means in terms of English pronunciation. This is the last of Bernstein's four works for solo and orchestra, the others being the Second Symphony (solo piano), the *Serenade* (solo violin), and the *Three Meditations from "Mass"* (solo cello). None of them are concertos in the conventional sense, but all four are, truly, concertos in the essential meaning of the term: "to strive together", to explore the relationship between the solo voice and the larger ensemble. The work is dedicated "To the Spirit of Yadin and to his Fallen Brothers," referring to nineteen-year-old Israeli flutist Yadin Tanenbaum, killed while serving in the Israeli army in the Sinai desert in 1973.

Formally speaking, *Halil* is a kind of cross between a symphonic poem and a concerto. Bernstein subtitles the piece "Nocturne for Solo Flute with Piccolo, Alto Flute, Percussion, Harp and Strings," adding, "it is a kind of night-music which, from its opening 12-tone row to its ambiguously diatonic final cadence, is an ongoing conflict of nocturnal images: wish-dreams, nightmares, repose, sleeplessness, night-terrors, and sleep itself, *Death's twin brother*." This program certainly leaves plenty of room for the creation of a single-movement, freeform rhapsody such as we find here. It's actually very interesting, given the literary or theatrical origins of virtually all of Bernstein's music, that he never actually wrote a self-avowed symphonic poem. This, plus *On the Waterfront*, are about as close as he got, and as you can see its program is even less literal than that of many of his more determinedly abstract instrumental works.

If you had a chance to read the section on the *Serenade*, then all the remarks I made there about the difficulty of writing violin concertos in matters of ensemble balance and stylistics apply doubly here. The flute, while traditionally the most popular member of the wind family for concerto treatment, has a sweetly charming but very limited expressive range, and a timbre that easily becomes fatiguing to the audience with extended listening. That's one reason it was so appropriate a choice of soloist in seemingly billions of short, fluffy, scrupulously tasteful baroque and rococo concertos that offer a few moments of bland pleasantness and absolutely nothing else. Bernstein, as you can see from his own description of the work, has quite another thing in mind, expressively speaking.

Many modern flute concertos make the soloist play not just the standard flute, but piccolo and alto flute as well to help relieve the timbral monotony. Bernstein has the best of both worlds, hiding those two other members of the same family within the percussion section to echo and intertwine with the soloist, and occasionally take center stage themselves. It works wonderfully well. The remainder of the ensemble, as in the *Serenade*, consists of harp, strings, and percussion. Indeed, this is such an effective combination for a modern concerto accompaniment (as Bernstein must have realized since he used it in all of his concerted works for melody instruments) that it deserves to be more generally adopted. At no point do we encounter any balance problems between the flute and the orchestra, and even at the loudest moments the timbre of the woodwind instrument is so different from everything else that it cuts right through without difficulty.

## GUIDE TO LISTENING

If Bernstein's reference to a twelve-note row in his description of *Halil* makes you nervous, don't be. In the first place, there's nothing wrong with twelve-tone (or serial) music as long as it's good music; most of it isn't, but that's another issue, and hardly a unique one. Bernstein's use of the technique always has an expressive purpose, and it's usually exactly what atonal music means to most people: fear, sadness, death, emptiness, and other creepy emotions. Also, it's worth pointing out that you really do have to work pretty hard to make anything sound truly unpleasant on a flute (though some modern composers have tried, and sometimes even succeeded). Like a small child unwittingly using foul language, the result is more likely to be cute, even charming, rather than offensive or obnoxious.

*Halil*, which lasts about sixteen minutes in all, begins adagio (very slowly) with a loud swoosh from the strings, harp, low and high gongs, and the vibraphone. It's a haunting sound entirely apt for the haunted music that follows. The flute enters immediately with its twelve-tone theme, a distinctive melody that wanders sadly above a softly percussive dreamscape. The alto flute, "distant," joins the soloist very shortly thereafter, and the two play a ghostly duet culminating in a return to the opening gesture. For the purposes of understanding the form of the piece, which isn't at all complicated, call this opening section A.

A short transition leads to B, a lyrical theme for the flute accompanied by the strings and harp. This music is sweetly tonal, but the atonal elements soon corrupt and distort it (listen for the reentry of the percussion—gongs and suspended cymbal). The strings protest passionately, and the flute interjects with an actual return to its opening gesture, fortissimo and "biting." Calm returns, as the violins once again sing out the B theme with the flute adding a new counterpoint above, but once again tonal instability gains the upper hand and carries the music to its first big climax (punctuated by the bass drum, snare drum, and glockenspiel). On the other side, the solo and alto flutes lead the decline into a moment of silence.

So far, the form of this first third of the piece has been very straightforward: ABABA. Now a brief "misterioso" passage on tremolo strings and harp leads to the central quick section, allegro con brio. After a powerful introduction for strings and percussion, the flute returns to lead a waltzlike dance, accompanied by harp, strings, and the four tom-toms. You may notice that the rhythm of the flute's phrases cuts across that of the dance, creating a certain tension that is very effective in keeping the music urgently propulsive. About halfway through this passage, the piccolo joins the soloist, lending an even more jocular character to the increasing energy. The music rushes to a big climax with snare drum rim shots, a huge crash on the tam-tam, and a bass drum roll. The percussion contributions spill over into a cadenza for flute soloist (the opening is marked "shrieking").

You may want to compare this cadenza to the "Masque" from the Second Symphony, or even the "Din Torah" from the "Kaddish" Symphony, which are similarly scored just for the soloist and percussion. Here again, this combination of instruments is remarkably effective in creating an atmospheric framework within which the solo flute can take center stage. Bernstein asks the flute to show off its entire range, both of expression and technical virtuosity, from "childlike" to "panting," "breathy," and eventually "more and more desperate." Toward the end the piccolo joins in briefly, and the solo climaxes on a viciously high tremolo (the technique is called "flutter tongue," which explains it all) under which the strings reenter with what is clearly a recapitulation of the opening music.

In fact, it's a recapitulation of the entire opening section, very abbreviated, and (interestingly) the solo flute does not participate, although both the alto flute and piccolo do. There is no final restatement of A; Bernstein believed in the positive qualities of tonality, and so the recapitulation of the lyrical B theme turns into a very brief coda that does indeed suggest sleep. At the very end, the solo flute enters to sound a final note that Bernstein says should be held "as long as possible." This conclusion, perhaps, does violate the first rule of traditional concerto writing, in that the soloist has little to do in the last few minutes following the cadenza. Perhaps this is why Bernstein, ever sensitive to such niceties, did not call *Halil* a concerto. On the other hand, the work remains a brilliant display piece for the soloist in all other respects, as well as an opportunity to enter a world of poetic feeling that few modern flutists can resist.

## Concerto for Orchestra ("Jubilee Games") (1989)

*Scoring: baritone solo, piccolo, 3 flutes, alto flute, 2 oboes, English horn, alto saxophone, E-flat clarinet, 2 clarinets, bass clarinet, 2 bassoons, contrabassoon, 4 horns, 3 trumpets, 3 trombones, tuba, vibraphone, xylophone, snare drum, tenor drum, bass drum, cymbals, tam-tam, 3 woodblocks, 5 tom-toms, anvil, triangle, cowbell, tambourine, chimes, harp, mandolin, piano, tape, and strings*

Bernstein's Concerto for Orchestra, his last completed work, built itself up over time. It began life in 1986 with two movements: the first and third of the current work. Bernstein then added the closing Benediction, and in 1988 the second movement variations. Originally commissioned for the fiftieth anniversary celebration of the Israel Philharmonic, the final version was also premiered by that orchestra in 1989. Those performance were recorded and issued on Deutsche Grammophon, and the work has received a couple of performance (and recordings) since. Still, it is too new to see if it has "legs." Certainly it represents Bernstein, in places at least, at his most experimental, but in other respects there are many familiar elements: the play of variations, the multiethnic dance music, and of course, the final benediction.

As currently constituted, the concerto has four movements:

1. "Free-Style Events"
2. "Mixed Doubles" (Theme and Seven Variations)
3. "Diaspora Dances"
4. "Benediction"

The proximate model for the work may have been Bartók's famous Concerto for Orchestra, particularly as the second movements in both pieces feature pairs of instruments in sequence, though Bartók's pairs are of the same kind whereas Bernstein's are not. Still, the brilliant writing for each orchestral section and the tendency to treat individual instruments as soloists, however briefly, more than justifies the "concerto" in the title.

## GUIDE TO LISTENING

### I. "Free-Style Events"

It is particularly difficult to describe a movement that never quite sounds the same twice. Bernstein has built into the overall structure, which is predetermined, a substantial chance element. Large tracts of music leave it up to the players to decide what they actually do. Still, the basis of the piece is a celebratory fanfare in which the orchestra shouts seven times the number seven, evoking the biblical commandment to celebrate a jubilee every forty-nine years (plus one equals the fifty years of the Israel Philharmonic in 1986). After the 7×7 business the players also yell "fifty" in Hebrew (*chamishim*). The music ranges from reckless brass fanfares and evocative imitations of the Jewish shofar (ram's horn) to a solemn chorale.

Some elements are taped and combined with the live orchestra as the music proceeds. The entire piece explodes with energy and, after seven high-voltage minutes, comes to a crashing close. This is the one movement, if any, that may limit the life of the work as a whole. After all, it doesn't make a lot of sense to continue shouting about the fiftieth anniversary of the Israel Philharmonic, especially if you aren't the Israel Philharmonic. Still, the problem (if it becomes one) is easily remedied by either changing the language, the numbers, or both, or by leaving the yelling out entirely. No one will miss it, I am sure, and Bernstein always ensures that music works first and foremost as music.

### 2. "Mixed Doubles" (Theme and Seven Variations)

Bernstein was a master variation writer, and this movement is no exception, though the very spare textures take some getting used to. This really is chamber music, and the instrumental combinations are sometimes very unusual and interesting. Every principal player in each orchestral section gets a solo in one of the variations (or in the coda). Because this is basically a slow movement, the theme is a sad, wistful melody on the strings. All of the variations are duets, and that means plenty of opportunities for simple counterpoint—canonic writing (one part follows another with the same music) or double variations played in combination. The instrumental pairings are:

a. Flute and horn: A variation that sticks close to the original melody in the horn, while the flute provides a decorative counterpoint.
b. Trumpet and double bass: A zippy canonic variation. First the trumpet leads, then when the bass plays pizzicato the roles reverse.
c. Clarinet and trombone: The clarinet has the theme, and while the trombone begins with the simplest of accompaniments, it keeps wanting to take command and finally blows the clarinet away with a very funny Bronx cheer.
d. Percussion: It's mallets versus drums and piano. Okay, Bernstein may be cheating a bit on the "doubles" concept here, but the music needs some fuller textures now and again, and this jaunty march offers just the ticket.
e. Two solo violins: A very busy variation for two solo violins in seemingly perpetual motion.
f. Alto flute and bass clarinet: These two lowest members of their respective families make a surprisingly effective team, offering a wistful and mellow transformation of the theme.
g. Oboe and bassoon: Another canonic variation, the two instruments chase each other, giving a gruff snort at the end of each phrase. This makes the counterpoint particularly easy to follow.

Coda: Solo cello and solo viola return with the original theme, and the movement ends with all of the soloists (except percussion) coming in together on the final note.

## 3. "Diaspora Dances"

The title speaks for itself. There's some more numerology at work here, mostly based on the numbers 9 and 18, the latter being the numerical value of the Hebrew letters that make up the word *life* (*chai*). The orchestra whispers the actual word at the opening of the movement. Bernstein was of course a great master at stylized ethnic dance music, and he presents here a whirlwind survey of the many styles of Jewish music that evolved around the world. It's brilliant, witty, tuneful, and oddly disorienting, all at the same time.

## 4. "Benediction"

The slow finale begins with another volley of brilliant brass fanfares, but the music settles down rapidly and the solo oboe plays the main theme, accompanied by a soulful counterpoint on the bassoon. The strings repeat the melody, gently and softly, its long arcs of melody rising high in the violins. Once the violins have finished, the baritone solo enters with the Benediction (in Hebrew):

> May the Lord bless you and keep you;
>
> May the Lord cause his face to shine upon you, and be gracious to you;
>
> May the Lord lift his gaze to you and grant you peace.

It's strange to think that when he conducted the final version of the Concerto for Orchestra, Bernstein had only a year to live. Obviously he didn't know that his days were numbered, but there's something fitting about his leaving us with a setting of this Benediction, ending on a bittersweet dissonance, gentle, yet mysteriously inconclusive.

# Overtures and Shorter Pieces

The works in this section may be classified as "chips off the master's workbench," but they reveal as polished a level of craftsmanship as anything in Bernstein's output. Like all serious artists, he recognized only two kinds of music, good and bad, and even in his slightest pieces he made sure that the end result lived up to his very high standards. The art of creating great "light" or occasional music tends to be sneered at by heavy duty classical music fans, critics, and scholars, quite unfairly. It's a gift, a major one, and an ability that Bernstein had in spades. Even he downplayed it to some extent; he wanted to take on big projects and produce major works about important issues, and of course he did that too, but it's still a good thing that he had the time and opportunity to write such a t errific group of pieces in this vein.

## Candide Overture (1956)

*Scoring: piccolo, 2 flutes, 2 oboes, E-flat clarinet, two clarinets, bass clarinet, 2 bassoons, contrabassoon, 4 horns, 3 trumpets, 3 trombones, tuba, snare drum, tenor drum, bass drum, cymbals, triangle, glockenspiel, xylophone, timpani, harp, and strings*

Only a tiny handful of great comic opera overtures are in the basic orchestral repertoire: Mozart's *The Marriage of Figaro* and *Così fan tutte*, Smetana's *The Bartered Bride*, Carl Nielsen's *Maskarade*, several by Rossini, and this one. By "comic," I mean that the music is as funny as the story itself. Thus, Wagner's prelude to *Die Meistersinger von Nürnberg* is unquestionably a great overture, but funny it most certainly is not. Bernstein's *Candide* Overture, on the other hand, is a hilarious concoction of witty melodies, scored with positively cartoonish glee. Although the musical (or "operetta") was composed as far back as 1956, the complete work didn't achieve its definitive form until 1989, a sure sign of just how important it was to Bernstein. Most of the issues concerned muscling the libretto into its optimal shape. The music was from the first acknowledged as masterful, but Bernstein, always the craftsman, tinkered with the orchestration until the very end as well.

## GUIDE TO LISTENING

Formally, the *Candide* overture is a brilliant cross between Mozart and Rossini, with the high kick of Offenbach tossed in for good measure. In other words, it's a sort of operetta overture on steroids, one that deploys every trick in the compositional book to capture the madcap high jinks of the story. The main body of the overture has exactly the same form as the overture to *The Marriage of Figaro*, what musicologists call "sonata form without development." What this means is actually quite simple: a first theme, a second theme in its complementary key, and then both of them get repeated by way of recapitulation in the opening key. There is no central development section. This keeps the piece short and removes any suggestion of more serious intent, which tends to happen when composers have to vary the main themes in numerous ways—some of which inevitably will compromise their initial, in this case ebullient, character.

*Candide* is also a potpourri overture, meaning that it quotes some of the big tunes to come later. This is something that neither Mozart nor Rossini did very often, but of course it's entirely typical of the prelude to a Broadway musical. The most important foreshadowing of music to come consists of:

1. The opening fanfare, which returns at various points in the action
2. The warmly lyrical and graceful second subject ("Oh Happy We")
3. The coda ("Glitter and Be Gay")

This last item calls for special mention. It's the Rossini bit, a real "Rossini crescendo" such as we find in such overtures as *The Barber of Seville*, *Cinderella*, or *The Thieving Magpie*.

Although it only plays for a bit more than four minutes and spends most of its time being funny, *Candide* has become Bernstein's musical calling card as a serious composer. The music works equally well at pops and regular subscription concerts as a curtain-raiser, and fabulously as an encore. It sounds great on your MP3 player while jogging or working out. The rhythmic tricks that Bernstein deploys in its main theme, its surge of cancanlike energy, the wacky writing for xylophone, the pompous brass, clucking strings and woodwinds (shades of Haydn's "Hen" Symphony), and the luscious romanticism of "Oh Happy We," have ensured that it remains a concert favorite. It also shows that great music need not be tragic, and that for Bernstein joy is just as deep an emotion as sorrow.

## A Musical Toast (1980)

*Scoring: 2 piccolos, 2 flutes, 2 oboes, E-flat clarinet, two clarinets, 2 bassoons, contrabassoon, 4 horns, 3 trumpets, 3 trombones, tuba, 4 snare drums, bass drum, cymbals, maracas, cymbals, triangle, woodblock, chimes, vibraphone, glockenspiel, xylophone, timpani, harp, piano, electric guitar (optional), organ (optional), and strings*

Some pieces are so much fun, you regret that they end so soon. *A Musical Toast* is one of these. Playing for just a bit shy of two minutes, and "fondly dedicated" to the memory of "pops" conductor André Kostelanetz, the entire piece is based on a motive that incorporates the rhythm of his name, but this isn't revealed immediately. As you can see, Bernstein asks for a very large orchestra (including kitchen-sink optional instruments), and sets out to make the most joyful noise possible. The work starts with a brazen fanfare leading to loud unison statement of "André Kostelanetz" by the full brass section. The music quiets down to the gentle rhythmic clicking of violas and cellos struck by the wooden backs of their bows (*col legno*).

The main theme is related to, but not quite the same as, the Kostelanetz motive. Even two minutes of music needs a real theme to carry it through, and this one is vintage Bernstein—the same Latin rhythm that we find in the dances from *West Side Story* and the central movement of the "Jeremiah" Symphony. After reaching a quick climax, the Kostelanetz motive returns, *grazioso* (graciously), on the woodwinds, as a tiny central interlude, leading to a full orchestral restatement of the main them. At its loudest point the orchestra breaks off abruptly and everyone sings the name "André Kostelanetz," giving the whole game away and racing on to the finish. The closing seconds feature a grand chorale, including the organ if one happens to be available, before slamming to a halt with "...telanetz."

*A Musical Toast* is, obviously, a very occasional work, but the point in discussing it in detail is to note, first, how typical of its composer even this little piece sounds, and second, how very characteristic of Bernstein writing tributes to his musical colleagues actually was. Especially as his activities as a conductor and teacher left him ever less time for composition, the opportunity to write a new work dedicated to fellow artist seemed to be something that Bernstein always found time for. Too slender for a normal concert (even at its premiere it was played through twice), *A Musical Toast* nevertheless makes a fine encore and, of course, a touching tribute to the memory of another splendid conductor.

## Slava! (1977)

*Scoring: piccolo, 2 flutes, 2 oboes, E-flat clarinet, two clarinets,*
*bass clarinet, soprano saxophone, 2 bassoons, contrabassoon,*
*4 horns, 3 trumpets, 3 trombones, tuba, 2 snare drums, tenor*

*drum, bass drum, cymbals, triangle, woodblock, tambourine, whip, ratchet, steel pipe, slide whistle, trap set, marimba, chimes, vibraphone, glockenspiel, xylophone, timpani, piano, electric guitar, tape, and strings*

Subtitled "A Political Overture," *Slava!* was composed for the inaugural season of Russian cellist/conductor Mstislav ("Slava") Rostropovich as music director of the National Symphony Orchestra of Washington, D.C. There's a bit of a back story here that's worth knowing, not for the musical light it sheds on the piece but because it's so interesting as history all by itself. In the early 1970s, Rostropovich and his wife, the Bolshoi Opera's leading soprano Galina Vishnevskaya, had been branded as dissidents in the USSR on account of their support for *Gulag Archipelago* author Aleksander Solzhenitsyn (among other reasons). They were effectively blacklisted in their own country, prevented from working or from traveling abroad.

As Vishnevskaya tells it in her autobiography, Bernstein was instrumental in helping to secure permission for them to leave the Soviet Union. He spoke to Senator Ted Kennedy, who was traveling to Moscow, about the plight of his friends, and the senator in turn asked Leonid Brezhnev personally to permit the family to leave. Permission was duly granted in 1974. On reaching the West, nominally for two years but in reality indefinitely, Rostropovich and Vishnevskaya were stripped of their Soviet citizenship in 1978 and branded as traitors to their own country. Rostropovich's appointment as music director of the National Symphony in Washington, D.C., undoubtedly was seen by the Russian authorities as a political statement, although as he was one of the twentieth-century's finest and most acclaimed musicians, there was no serious question about his qualifications for the job.

So Russia's loss was America's gain, not just because it put the National Symphony Orchestra on the musical map (culminating in the recording of an excellent cycle of Shostakovich symphonies, among other projects), but it resulted in the creation of this racy and hilarious overture. Although ostensibly a short, occasional piece, *Slava!* actually is the same length as the *Candide* Overture, at least in Bernstein's own recording. A footnote in the score, however, recommends that the piece be used not as a concert opener, but to provide a rousing conclusion, or even as an encore. This concern for placement suggests that, although short, the piece mattered to Bernstein, as well it should. It's very good music, and clearly Bernstein lavished no small amount of care in its creation.

## GUIDE TO LISTENING

Although the entire overture breezes by in one basic tempo, "fast and flamboyant," it contains two highly contrasted thematic complexes. The first is a riotous potpourri of early twentieth-century political propaganda "fight" songs, scored mostly for brass. "Wah-wah" and "growl" mutes as well as jazz playing techniques (shakes, tremolos, glissandos, and suchlike) combine with "oompah" percussion to produce a glitzy, roaring-twenties atmosphere. The second theme is a catchy, lyrical melody in Bernstein's characteristic Latin compound rhythm, very cleverly scored for soprano saxophone and electric guitar. Bernstein developed a great fondness for the electric guitar in his later music, in common with many contemporary composers. However, few use it as effectively as Bernstein does here.

The same observation applies to what happens next. After a raucous climax, a series of taped excerpts from overlapping political speeches mix with crowd noises, all over a constant rhythm in the trap set and piano, leading to a triumphant, "I give you . . . the next president of the United States of America!" As with the electric guitar, innumerable pieces of contemporary music use taped sounds, but the number that do it well, that justify their inclusion as musically (never mind as humorously) as Bernstein does here, is vanishingly small. The taped episode only lasts about thirty seconds, just long enough to make its witty point without becoming irritating.

This episode does double duty as the overture's development section, and immediately afterward the main themes return, only rescored and in reverse order. The opening sounds almost dainty as arranged for piano and solo strings, but then the rest of the orchestra wakes up and rushes to a rousing climax. The trombones at the end belt out a few bars of the famous "Slava" (it means "glory") chorus from Mussorgsky's opera *Boris Godunov*—in the Latin rhythm of the second theme, no less—then the players shout out, "Slava!" and the overture closes with a crash. Why the piece isn't better known is a completely mystery.


## *Prelude, Fugue, and Riffs* (1949)

*Scoring: solo clarinet, 2 alto saxophones (1 doubling clarinet),*
*  2 tenor saxophones, baritone saxophone, 5 trumpets,*
*  4 trombones, 4 tom-toms, traps, xylophone, vibraphone,*
*  woodblock, timpani, piano, and string bass*

Bernstein knew so much about music of all kinds that it's interesting to speculate on the kind of composer he might have been had his focus not been centered on the classical repertoire. *Mass* gives us some idea of him in rock, and the influence of jazz permeates his music of all periods. This, however, is his only piece of "pure" jazz, and while the melodic idiom certainly fits that description, the form of the piece is, at least in part, classical. Bernstein would turn to the prelude and fugue again in his *Serenade*, also in a distinctive way. The form is famous as it was used by Bach in many of his organ pieces, and most memorably in his *Well-Tempered Clavier*, forty-eight preludes and fugues in all the major and minor keys (two in each).

This updating of Bach to modern times was certainly not unusual, even in 1949. Villa-Lobos had been doing it for years in his famous series of *Bachianas Brasileiras*, combining baroque formal procedures with Brazilian folk melodies, and jazz musicians themselves have always found Bach a fount of inspiration for their own work. Bernstein wrote *PF&R* (for short) originally for Woody Herman, but his band broke up and so it was premiered by Benny Goodman on television in 1955, and dedicated to him as well. But Bach isn't the only inspiration here: Stravinsky also looms large. The Russian composer's *Ebony Concerto* had been premiered by Herman in 1946, but Bernstein's brass writing in the Prelude looks back further still, to the same composer's *Symphonies of Wind Instruments*, composed in 1920 but revised in 1947. Both the

Stravinsky and the Bernstein last almost exactly the same amount of time: about nine minutes.

The form of *PF&R* is both simple and ingenious. The prelude presents two major ideas; the fugue uses them as its subjects; and the riffs section introduces a solo clarinet with new material, primarily rhythmic, atop which all the other themes and motives return to make a grand finale. The presence of the solo clarinet suggests that this might also be considered one of Bernstein's "concerto" pieces, like the Second Symphony, the *Serenade*, *Halil*, or the *Three Meditations*, but since the clarinet only plays in the third movement, it's better to think of its role as "first among equals" rather than as a true concerto soloist.

## GUIDE TO LISTENING

All three movements run into each other without pause. The prelude has a straightforward ABA structure, and is scored for brass and percussion. Its main idea is a sort of trumpet fanfare, followed by a muted (literally) answer. The central section is a bit of dirty jazz, a slow "drag" accompanied by adlibbing rock rhythms on the trap set. The opening idea returns briefly, and continues on directly into the fugue. Here the saxophones take over and have the movement to themselves. This is actually a double fugue, meaning that it has two themes, or subjects. The first clearly derives from the opening trumpet call; the second, presented a bit later, is a smooth, lyrical phrase in even rhythm. Both of these themes are combined, and then the solo clarinet enters with the piano for the concluding riffs.

A riff is simply a repeated melodic figure, and that's exactly what the clarinet offers. Both the clarinet and piano take turns swapping riffs on jazzy bits of melody, and then Bernstein starts building his final climax with the return of material from the previous two movements. There's a very funny moment toward the end—when the xylophone enters with the original clarinet riffs—that sounds strangely like a jazz version of Salome's "Dance of the Seven Veils," a point of comparison that Bernstein undoubtedly would have noted and found very amusing. Beyond that, the music is exuberantly direct, exhilarating, and punchy straight through to its conclusion.

## Divertimento (1980)

*Scoring: 2 piccolos, 3 flutes, 2 oboes, English horn, E-flat*
  *clarinet, 2 clarinets, bass clarinet, 2 bassoons, contrabassoon,*
  *4 horns, 3 trumpets, 3 trombones, tuba, baritone euphonium,*
  *4 snare drums, bass drum, cymbals, tam-tam, triangle,*
  *tambourine, woodblock, 2 Cuban cowbells, sandpaper blocks,*
  *rasp, maracas, 3 bongos, 2 conga drums, 4 temple blocks, trap*
  *set, glockenspiel, vibraphone, xylophone, chimes, timpani,*
  *piano, harp, and strings*

Arguably the masterpiece of Bernstein's last decade, the *Divertimento* is simply one of the funniest pieces of concert music in existence, and the more you know about the various styles and genres that it parodies (always affectionately), the funnier it sounds. A *divertimento* is a musical diversion, a piece of light entertainment. In the eighteenth century, from whence the term derives, it was used interchangeably with *nocturne, cassation, serenade, partita,* or any other word that describes music designed to be played outdoors, under a balcony, during a dinner, or as accompaniment to a pleasurable pastime. Naturally the best exemplars were intended—by the composers at least—actually to be listened to, and Bernstein's music is certainly as artful as it is diverting. Indeed, it's impossible to ignore.

By 1980, when this piece appeared, there was a general sense that Bernstein had written himself out as a composer. New works appeared sporadically, and enjoyed only limited success. Even this one had detractors who claimed that it represented little more than facile pastiche. The truth is that by this period Bernstein the composer really couldn't win. To the extent he employed twelve-tone or other modernist techniques, he was trying anxiously to gain respectability as a serious composer among the academic avant-garde. But if he wrote in his most popular vein, he was pandering to the lowest common denominator of the listening public.

*Divertimento*, to a certain extent, answers both of these criticisms, and does so with the musical equivalent of a resounding Bronx cheer. It was a huge success at its premiere performances (one of which I was fortunate enough to attend) with the Boston Symphony Orchestra for whose centennial it was composed. It has remained popular ever since. The BSO was Bernstein's "first" orchestra, his home-town team, as it were. Critics of Bernstein's late works, especially those written for particular performers such as Rostropovich (*Three Meditations, Slava!*), Jean-Pierre Rampal (*Halil*), the Israel Philharmonic (Concerto for Orchestra), or the BSO as here, seldom stop to ask themselves if Bernstein would ever "write down" to his colleagues, or offer them less than his best efforts. The answer, hopefully, is self-evident.

What distinguishes the divertimento or serenade genre from pieces such as symphonies or concertos is the presence of extra movements, usually slow ones, or dances. Bernstein gives us a bit of both, updating the dance numbers to take in such post-eighteenth-century developments such as the samba, as well as the raunchiest blues movement that he (or anyone else) ever penned. All told, there are eight movements lasting just about fifteen minutes, making the *Divertimento* a perfect concert opener for any program featuring a large enough orchestra.

## GUIDE TO LISTENING

### First Movement: Sennets and Tuckets

All of the music in the *Divertimento* is based on a tiny motto: the notes B and C, which stand for "Boston Centennial." By itself this is so innocuous as to be effectively lost in the larger array of thematic material, but if you want to hear it, pay attention to the first entry of the violins (with horns and trumpets) in the third bar of the first movement, right after the rim shot on the snare drum. The first note of the bar is played pizzicato, and you may not hear it, but the following four (two eighth notes, then two quartet notes in a rising phrase) are bowed, and the last two of those (the quarter notes) contain the B–C motto. After that, just forget about it. I'll mention it wherever it matters.

"Sennets and tuckets" is the Shakespearian term for "fanfares," and that's just what Bernstein gives us: a brassy celebration that eventually settles down to a comical bit of tune backed by an oompah rhythm in the bass drum and snare drums. And that's the essence of the movement: a brilliant introduction to everything that follows; but as you will soon hear, its main theme has an important role to play later on. So the large-scale unity of the work doesn't depend entirely on the presence of the B–C motto alone; it's both deeper and more readily audible than that.

## Second Movement: Waltz

Scored for strings only, this is without question one of the wackiest waltzes in the entire orchestral repertoire. First, there's the melody: it's the Minuet in G Major from J. S. Bach's *Little Notebook for Anna Magdalena Bach*. It's one of those pieces that every kid studying the piano (including yours truly) learns at one point; and even if you didn't play a keyboard instrument you may well find the melody familiar. But it seems to have acquired a limp: the meter is 7/8 rather than the usual 3/4, and so while the music evidently wants to be a waltz, it keeps tripping over its own feet as it proceeds. All the usual clichés of the Viennese style are here: the succulent glissandos, yummy vibrato timbres, elastic tempos, the affected elegance; and that only makes the music even funnier.

## Third Movement: Mazurka

This soulful excursion to Eastern Europe features the double reeds (oboes, English horn, bassoons, and contrabassoon), plus the harp. Aside from a couple of 5/4 bars, this piece sticks to its dance rhythm. Bernstein has a joke of another kind in store toward the end, when the first oboe breaks free to indulge in its famous solo from the recapitulation of Beethoven's Fifth Symphony's first movement. Like all good musical jokes, if you get it, then it's a bonus. If not, the music works perfectly well on its own terms, and you really don't have to know anything beyond what you actually hear as it occurs.

## Fourth Movement: Samba

We've come a goodly distance from the eighteenth-century divertimento in style, if not in spirit, when this racy Latin number erupts with all the usual percussive accoutrements: bongos, congas, rasp (guiro), maracas, and couple of Cuban cowbells for good measure. I've already mentioned several times just how pervasive the Latin influence on

Bernstein's music was, whether he's evoking the style specifically, or merely adopting its characteristic rhythmic syntax to his own uses. The Samba is actually relatively straightforward, rhythmically speaking (it's in 2/2), so the emphasis here is on the melody, and the sonorities of the brass and percussion. This movement may also represent an affectionate tribute to Bernstein's colleague and fellow composer, Morton Gould, a master of light music, whose *Latin American Symphonette* it strikingly resembles.

### Fifth Movement: "Turkey Trot"

This irresistible number also features a tune you'll swear you've heard somewhere, and the setting, with four temple blocks and a woodblock tick-tocking away, couldn't be more adorable. Leroy Anderson, eat your heart out! There's also a middle section of equal charm, but this being the midpoint of the work, the theme is a more fully realized version of the principal tune from the opening movement. So the piece serves a genuine formal purpose, in addition to being the number that usually gets encored either at the end of the work, or of the concert. It's easy to make fun of this corny bit of Americana, but the ability to write this sort of tune, and write it well, is still one of the greatest gifts a composer can ask for.

### Sixth and Seventh Movements: "Sphinxes" and "Blues"

The next two movements are connected. "Sphinxes," aside from suggesting the famous riddle of Greek mythology, also refers to the similarly named number in Schumann's *Carnival* for piano, a collection of character vignettes very similar in its own way to what Bernstein does in his *Divertimento*. Schumann's "Sphinxes" consist of three melodic mottos, two of four notes, one of three notes, on which the remaining pieces are based. There's an ongoing controversy as to whether or not he intended that they actually be played. Bernstein's "Sphinxes" consist of two twelve-note rows, one played by the strings, then the winds, each ending in a tonal cadence. The ending is the joke, but it's an inside one, Bernstein's wry commentary on the enduring values of tonal music.

The "Blues" that follows is, as previously suggested, one of the most raunchy jazz movements in any avowedly "classical" piece. Bernstein scores it for three trumpets, three trombones, euphonium, tuba, trap set, vibraphone, and piano. Like the waltz, the music takes the style to the limit: the various muted brass sonorities, "wailing" techniques, vibrato, sizzle cymbal, brushes on the trap set—it's all there. The movement closes with a wonderfully evocative cadenza for solo trumpet, and a soft riff on the drums.

### Eighth Movement: "In Memoriam"; March: "The BSO Forever"

This finale also contains two connected parts. First, there's a memorial to departed members of the BSO in the form of a canon (a round) for three flutes. This tiny elegy starts off with the B–C motive in perhaps its most clearly audible form: for the first couple of measures the flute warbles back and forth on the two notes. The melody reaches a natural climax, increasing in volume and pitch with the entrance of each flute. At the end, it spills over into the march, a goofy take off on Sousa's *The Stars and Stripes Forever*. The melody is that of the first movement and the middle section of "Turkey Trot," forced into a shape suspiciously similar to that of Johann Strauss Sr.'s famous *Radetzky March*.

There are two contrasting sections, or *trios* as they're called in the march business. The second, played by the winds, has the parts marked "dumbly," "stupidly," "imbecilically," and "cretinously" respectively. There's an obligatory descant for piccolos, whose players get to stand up for it, and then the entire brass section rises to its feet for the final peroration. After the premiere, in 1985, Bernstein reworked the final pages to add an additional reprise of the second trio before the concluding free-for-all, but his recording predates the revision. So, as fine as his recording is, if you want to hear his last thoughts on the piece (and they do represent an improvement in that they give the march a touch more size and substance), consider any one of the number of excellent alternatives.

# Vocal and Choral Music

Most of Bernstein's major works have a vocal component, including two of his three symphonies, but aside from his musicals and operas the number of major choral/vocal concert works is quite small: just these two pieces. They are, however, important ones. Bernstein was a master at writing for the voice, not something to be taken for granted, particularly in contemporary music which has largely forgotten or ignored the fact that for centuries the basis of all instrumental writing has been to imitate the natural expressiveness of the human singing voice. Bernstein accepted this tradition, and reveled in it. Over the course of his career he set texts in several languages, including English, Spanish, Hebrew, and Latin, always with what seems like effortless mastery. Three of these languages (all except Latin) feature in the two works considered in this chapter, and taken together they offer a clinic in the art of text-setting and vocal composition.

## Chichester Psalms (1965)

*Scoring: male alto, choir, 3 trumpets, 3 trombones, glockenspiel, xylophone, chimes, triangle, woodblock, temple blocks, tambourine, snare drum, 3 bongos, bass drum, cymbals, whip, rasp, timpani, 2 harps, and strings*

Bernstein wrote relatively few stand-alone pieces for choir and orchestra (apart from stage works). There's this one, and the Third Symphony of two years previously. The contrast between them couldn't be greater. His "Kaddish" Symphony remains his ultimate expression of metaphysical angst, whereas the *Psalms* are almost uniformly confident, hopeful, joyous, and contented. Of course the mood of each is dictated primarily by the selection of texts, but also because the *Psalms* were intended to be sung by church (and synagogue) choirs everywhere. While the symphony requires some pretty advanced choral techniques and training, this piece presents no special difficulties, even to a good amateur chorus. It also exists in two versions, a "practical" one for chorus, organ, harp, and percussion; and the one listed here, in which the organ part is taken over by brass and strings.

So depending on the version chosen, the *Chichester Psalms* has one foot in and one foot out of the larger pool of Bernstein's orchestral works. Nevertheless, it's worth considering here because of the numerous stylistic affinities that these three movements have with so much of the other music in this book. It can't be emphasized strongly enough that like all major composers, Bernstein had a musical style that was uniquely his own and which he adapted to suit whatever the circumstances required of him. This may be religious music, but its style is pure Bernstein, and by some standards resolutely secular in terms of energy and sonority. In this respect he was no different than Haydn, for whom being "religious" meant writing the best music possible by staying true to his own God-given talent.

Although nominally writing this for performance in an Anglican cathedral, Bernstein set the texts of these psalms in their original Hebrew, and that is how they are always performed. The texts, as you will see, were deliberately chosen to be as universal and nonsectarian as possible. This, too, has helped to ensure the work's enduring popularity—that, and the fact that it's really great fun to sing. The overall expressive trajectory of the three movements, from rambunctious high spirits, to a threatened peace, to inner calm, is beautifully organized to drive home the message of the closing chorale, from Psalm 133: "How good and how pleasant it is for brothers to live together in unity." For Bernstein, his life as a musician had no higher purpose than to express this creed.

## GUIDE TO LISTENING

### First Movement: Psalm 108:2; Psalm 100

As with all music that sets a text, the best way to listen is either to read the words and let it rip, or to follow them as they are sung. There's no particular need to quote the various psalms here in full, aside from a general discussion of the actual music. Many of Bernstein's more jubilant works start with a brief, preludial fanfare, and this one is no exception. Here the fanfare has words, taken from the second verse of Psalm 108: "Awake, harp and psaltery: I will awaken the dawn." Marked "majestically and energetically," like many of Bernstein's fanfares this one features constantly changing meters (6/4, 3/4, 3/8, 5/4, 2/4, 5/8 in the first half-dozen bars), and this serves to enhance the music's rhythmic swing when it finally settles down to its main pulse.

In this particular case, that pulse is 7/4, one of Bernstein's patented Latin rhythms: the classic prior case of a seven-beat meter can be found in the lilting "Pantomine" in 7/8 from Manuel de Falla's ballet *El amor brujo* (Love, the Magician). Bernstein is considerably more hard-driving. The tempo increases to Allegro molto for a setting of Psalm 100, a celebratory text beginning with the words, "Make a joyful noise unto the Lord, all ye peoples," and continuing in a similar vein. The entire movement is a three-and-a-half-minute paean of praise, filled to the brim with the celebratory sounds of brass and tuned percussion (bells, glockenspiel, xylophone), with the bongos thrown in to confirm the music's Jewish/Latin hybrid flavor.

I mentioned that the sound of this movement is determinedly secular. In fact, the other Bernstein piece that comes closest to this one in feeling, rhythm, and sonority is *A Musical Toast*, his two-minute tribute to conductor André Kostelanetz. Aside from one quiet interlude just before the end at the words, "For the Lord is good, His mercy everlasting," the entire movement flies by in a single impulsive sweep.

### Second Movement: Psalm 23; Psalm 2:1–4

The opening harp arpeggio, backed by suspended cymbal and triangle, gives this setting of the Twenty-third Psalm ("The Lord is my shepherd,

I shall not want . . .") a curiously exotic quality, almost like the opening violin solo in Rimsky-Korsakov's *Scheherazade*. For most of this tranquil text, expressive of simple faith, Bernstein asks for the relatively pure, vibratoless sound of a boy soprano or countertenor, but he supports the soloist with the women's voices from the choir. The melody and texture at the choral entry strongly foreshadow the lyrical, tonal melody in *Halil*, composed over a decade later. The first half of the psalm, up to "Thy rod and Thy staff, they comfort me," flows tranquilly on, with a lovely effect created by having the women hum as the soloist repeats the first line.

Psalm 2 interrupts this oasis of calm rudely, in a quicker tempo. The first line of text, "Why do the nations rage?" explains the music's bellicosity. Bernstein gives these lines to the men, appropriately, assisted by the brass and the more warlike percussion: snare drum, wood block, rasp (guiro), and whip. Most of the music proceeds at a whisper, albeit with sudden outbursts. Atop this, the women reenter with the second half of Psalm 23, and the two different kinds of music are combined, all at a subdued dynamic level. The treble soloist and the women's voices finish their psalm by themselves, but the orchestra slips in a few references to war at the very end, bringing the movement to a close with a startlingly loud thud.

### Third Movement: Psalm 131; Psalm 133:1

The third movement begins with an extended, slow orchestral prelude primarily for the strings, quite similar in tone to the passionate exordium at the start of the finale of the *Serenade*. As the music settles down, tenors and basses enter with the opening of Psalm 131, however, the text that best determines the character of the music comes from the middle of the poem: "Surely I have calmed and quieted myself, like a child that has been weaned from his mother, my soul is like that of weaned child." After the conflict of the previous movement, which presents as irreconcilable opposites pure trust in God and earthly strife, the 131st Psalm speaks of the self-willed return to faith and hope.

Although the longest movement of the three (about nine minutes), this one is the easiest to describe, since from the point that the choir enters the music proceeds in a single arch of warm, confident melody, slowly fading away at the end until the choir sings, as an unaccompanied chorale, the first line of Psalm 133 (already quoted) in praise of universal brotherhood. The expressive curve of the piece couldn't be clearer: sadness and despair, followed by calm faith (not easily won), making possible peace on earth among all peoples. It's a beautiful vision cloaked in some of Bernstein's most straightforwardly beautiful music.

At the same time, however, he's careful that this evocation of paradise never turns mawkish. "Non-sentimental," he cautions the singers, telling us (and them) to treat the text simply, just as Mahler cautions the singer in the finale of his Fourth Symphony to perform "without parody" in describing the heavenly life as seen through the eyes of a child. It's actually very interesting to note how frequently Bernstein, supposedly one of the twentieth century's most heart-on-sleeve artists, asks his performers to render his music without excessive sentimentality, and to let it speak plainly. In this respect he is very much a composer working in the Stravinsky/Copland/Hindemith neoclassical aesthetic, one that seeks to let the feelings in the music speak without undue exaggeration.

## Songfest (1977)

*Scoring: soprano, mezzo-soprano, alto, tenor, baritone, and bass soloists, piccolo, 3 flutes, 2 oboes, English horn, E-flat clarinet, 2 clarinets, bass clarinet, 2 bassoons, contrabassoon, 4 horns, 3 trumpets, 3 trombones, tuba, 3 snare drums, tenor drum, bass drum, cymbals, finger cymbals, sleigh bells, anvil, tam-tam, triangle, tambourine, woodblocks, rasp, maracas, 3 tom-toms, 3 rock drums, traps, glockenspiel, vibraphone, xylophone, chimes, timpani, harp, piano, celesta, electric keyboard, Fender bass, and strings*

The continued neglect of *Songfest* truly puzzles me. Perhaps the problem is logistics: it's hard to get six excellent singers together, because not only do they have individual numbers, they have to rehearse as an ensemble in sextets, duets, and trios. Nor is the music easy; Bernstein was a supreme professional writing for fellow professionals, and although he always took care to measure the capabilities of those he was writing for, as time wore on this mattered less and less. Still, he was undoubtedly one of the great song-writers of the twentieth century, and *Songfest* contains twelve marvelous songs to texts by as many major American poets.

In creating this piece, Bernstein had several models to look to for inspiration. First, there was Mahler's song-symphony *Das Lied von der Erde*, the example for all of the many, similar pieces that came after, and a work Bernstein knew and loved like few others (he recorded it twice). Also high on the list was Shostakovich's Fourteenth Symphony, which Bernstein also recorded. He composed *Songfest* ostensibly for the American bicentennial in 1976. However, it was not finished in time so the original commission was vacated, and Bernstein went on to complete the work anyway, a year late, fascinated with the prospect of paying musical tribute to more than three hundred years of American poetry.

You may be pleased to know that there are no overriding formal considerations to take into account when listening to *Songfest*. It is simply an eclectic mixture of styles and idioms, both poetic and musical. Bernstein satisfies any structural concerns through the method by which the poems are arranged, in six distinct parts:

1. Sextet
2. Three solos
3. Three ensembles (duet, trio, duet)
4. Sextet
5. Three solos
6. Sextet

Because these are songs, the best way to approach the piece is simply to sit down with the words and listen, so the descriptions below merely mention some of the musical highlights, starting with the identity of each of the poems.

## GUIDE TO LISTENING

### I. Sextet

*Songfest* begins with a characteristic celebratory fanfare. Rolling snare and tenor drums support declamatory brass in setting the stage for Frank O'Hara's "To the Poem." The singers announce: "Let us do something grand," and the music echoes the sentiment.

### 2. Three Solos

#### a. Lawrence Ferlinghetti: "The Pennycandystore Beyond the El" (baritone)

A blues setting that Bernstein marks to be played and sung "like a quick, dark dream," the music tells of a first (or last) love, and makes the mention of licorice sticks and Tootsie Rolls sound positively pornographic. The use of sizzle cymbal throughout the entire song gives the music an entirely apt, brittle chill.

#### b. Julia de Burgos: "A Julia de Burgos" (soprano)

This setting, in the original Spanish, of Puerto Rican poet Julia de Burgos's battle cry for women's liberation is a sort of apotheosis of Bernstein's Latin manner, and a tribute to everything he loved about it: the lilting rhythms in compound meters (7/8 and 5/8 abound), the brassy trumpet writing, and the virile percussion. As I noted in the Introduction, the Latin influence on Bernstein seldom gets its due in the critical literature, but it was very major, and it's difficult not to imagine here a possible hommage to his wife, Felicia Montealegre, as passionate a personality (by all accounts) as the poet herself.

#### c. Walt Whitman: "To What You Said" (bass)

Only discovered and published long after his death, this Walt Whitman poem deals tenderly with the subject of his homosexuality, and the relevance to Bernstein personally is obvious. Although this is nominally a bass solo, the other singers hum along in counterpoint with the soloist, while the orchestra anchors the melody with the note C throughout. The tune is one of Bernstein's most affecting.

## 3. Three Ensembles

### a. Langston Hughes: "I, Too, Sing America" (baritone); June Jordan: "Okay 'Negroes'" (mezzo-soprano)

This brilliant duet contrasts Langston Hughes's famous poem setting forth the claim of African Americans to equal rights and participation in American society (declaimed in broken rhythms), with an exaggeratedly jazzy setting of June Jordan's mocking picture of the assimilated "American Negro."

### b. Anne Bradstreet: "To My Dear and Loving Husband" (soprano, mezzo-soprano, alto)

The oldest poem in the cycle (Bradstreet lived from 1612 to '72), this lovely trio for three women's voices speaks plainly and simply of the poet's affection for her husband. There is not a trace of cynicism in this setting, nor the excess of sentimentality suggested by the text (a problem Bernstein believed he managed to avoid by setting the poem as a trio).

### c. Gertrude Stein: "Storyette H. M." (soprano, bass)

Stein's poem deals with the subject of a marriage between two incompatible people, one of whom seems to have been the painter Henri Matisse (the "H. M." of the title). Bernstein's setting is a light, breezy, tuneful little narrative song in which the two singers give a deadpan (Bernstein's direction) account of what seems to be a miserable situation.

## 4. Sextet

e. e. cummings's delicious little poem "if you can't eat you got to" offers the basic message (if I may paraphrase): "we ain't got nothing, not even death, so let's go to sleep." It elicits from Bernstein an equally piquant, scherzolike setting made all the more meaningful by being set as a sort of call-and-response number between all of the soloists. Passion breaks in at the climax, but the agitation subsides as the singers take the poet's advice and go to sleep, but not without a sly wink in the form of an explosive *p* (as in sleeP!) on the very last note.

## 5. Three Solos

### a. Conrad Aiken: "Music I Heard with You" (mezzo-soprano)

This lament for a lost love alternates tonal melodic and twelve-tone sections. The melody is almost identical to the lyrical theme that Bernstein uses in *Halil*, his nocturne for flute and orchestra. The twelve-tone sections feature delicate washes of color from the harp and celesta, and like all of Bernstein's use of serial techniques there is no threat of incompatibility between the two styles. The music remains all of a piece.

### b. Gregory Corso: "Zizi's Lament" (tenor)

God only knows what this one's about, but it's wonderful. The poem is a bitter lament about not having the "laughing sickness" like the speaker's other North African (Moroccan?) relatives. Now technically, *laughing sickness* is the common name for kuru, an illness similar to mad cow disease, first identified in Papua New Guinea in the 1950s, believed to be transmitted by human cannibalism. Somehow I don't think this is what Gregory Corso had in mind—or maybe he did. But it doesn't matter because the music is a wickedly sardonic belly dance, complete with finger cymbals, doleful bassoon, and plenty of maniacal laughter in the vocal line.

### c. Edna St. Vincent Millay: "What Lips My Lips Have Kissed" (alto)

The most sad, even tragic, song in the cycle, the poem speaks of the desolation of forgotten love in music of almost unbearable eloquence.

## 6. Sextet

Edgar Allan Poe's "Israfel," billed by Bernstein as a "closing hymn," is the Muslim spirit of music who, according to the Koran, will blow the trumpet on the Day of Judgment. Bernstein's setting is an ebullient waltz that gives each of the singers a moment to shine, with plenty of vocal display as well. According to Poe, Israfel particularly despises "an unimpassioned song," something that certainly can't be said of any of the pieces in *Songfest*!

As you can see from the astonishing range of material that Bernstein chose to set, *Songfest* encompasses, within the frame of the American experience, those issues of deepest significance to him: love, social justice, and the difficulty of establishing meaningful relationships. But it is also, perhaps first and foremost, a celebration of music, of Bernstein's joy in music, and of the culture that provided him with so much different music to absorb, imitate, and integrate. Hopefully, in time, *Songfest* will be recognized as the superlative work that it undoubtedly is.

# Ballets and Suites

ernstein's ballets and suites number among his most popular works. Although they don't ignore the more serious issues that he tackles so directly in his original concert pieces with text, the need to address a story nonverbally in terms of rhythm and melody means, ironically, that you could argue that these theatrical scores are more "absolute" than his actual symphonies. Bernstein was certainly aware of this. The ballets are wholly symphonic in construction, and the word *symphonic* itself appears in more than a few titles of the suites. He understood that any piece of music, no matter what its ostensible genre, needs to find its own satisfying form, and that the impact and power of musical expression is as dependent on structure (that is, on contrast, repetition, and variation) as it is on melody.

## *Fancy Free* (1944)

*Scoring: piccolo, 2 flutes, 2 oboes, 2 clarinets, 2 bassoons, 4 horns, 3 trumpets, 3 trombones, tuba, snare drum, bass drum, cymbals, triangle, woodblock, cowbell, timpani, piano, and strings*

The idea of a "symphonic" ballet was not new in 1944. After all, in the first years of the twentieth-century Ravel had already dubbed his *Daphnis et Chloë* a "choreographic symphony." What was new in Bernstein's *Fancy Free*, however, was the combination of a symphonic approach to the entire work with a contemporary subject that gave the composer the freedom to apply the technique to popular music idioms. Ravel's ballet evoking ancient Greece is all Ravel: There are no tangos, mazurkas, or waltzes, never mind Latin numbers or jazz. What Bernstein's early works show is that any style of music serves as fair game for a composer with the imagination and flair to use it well.

Only two years previously, Bernstein had burst on the scene as a composer with his "Jeremiah" Symphony. Both that work and *Fancy Free* show him perfecting his technique of "evolving variation," creating large-scale forms in which a section or movement generates material for the next one. This turns out to be an excellent way to achieve unity in a piece such as *Fancy Free*, in which the actual sequence of numbers is necessarily dictated by an external plot, and where the music has to fulfill a practical, in this case choreographic, purpose as well. The result is a ballet which functions equally as a concert piece, and which has no "dead spots," as even, say, Stravinsky's famous early ballets sometimes do. There is no conflict between theatrical necessity and symphonic process.

A comprehensive and reasonably objective history of twentieth-century music has yet to be written. We are still too close to the period in question to see it whole, and to weigh the significance of its various components. What is clear, however, from this vantage point is that ballet played a major role in musical progress in the hands of composers such as Stravinsky and Aaron Copland. Before the twentieth century, and with a few noteworthy French and Russian exceptions (principally Delibes and Tchaikovsky), ballet was a field for musical conservatives, bound by tradition and convention. After Stravinsky, the dance became a generator of musical progress, a tool of experiment, and a weapon of the avant-garde. It was Bernstein's good fortune that he was able to participate fully in this new paradigm, and *Fancy Free* should be seen in this context.

The plot of the ballet, which also served as the source for the musical *On the Town* (to completely different music), falls into seven distinct sections:

1. "Enter Three Sailors"
2. Scene at the Bar

3. "Enter Two Girls"
4. Pas de Deux
5. Competition Scene
6. Three Dance Variations: Galop, Waltz, Danzón
7. Finale

The story, as the titles suggest, concerns three sailors during war-time who come to New York on shore leave. They show up at a bar, looking to meet some girls. Finding two, they interact, compete for their attention, lose them, and run off after a third. The ballet originally began (and on recordings sometimes still does) with a jukebox blues number that Bernstein wrote for the occasion, called "Big Stuff." This song provides material for the Pas de Deux, but nothing gets lost musically if you haven't heard "Big Stuff" in advance.

## GUIDE TO LISTENING

### 1. "Enter Three Sailors"

If the performance includes "Big Stuff," the opening number interrupts the song at some point. Otherwise, four rim-shots on the snare drum introduce the three sailors with maximum energy and swagger. The first musical motive that you hear, six notes in jazzy rhythm from the trumpets and trombone, serves as the source for a lot of the music to follow. Pay special attention to the falling motto generated out of the last three notes of this theme (in its final form it has four notes), as well as to the important part given to the solo piano. The entire movement evolves out of this opening in a very striking example of Bernstein's ability to generate large forms through an endless play of variations on a few simple ideas.

### 2. Scene at the Bar

This reflective interlude starts with a long, slow, lyrical melody in the clarinets. As you can hear, it includes the descending, four-note motto, as does the expressive violin theme that follows. Note how Bernstein makes sure in these opening scenes that the basic musical ideas are repeated frequently enough so that they become firmly established in the listener's memory. Throughout this piece, the piano plays a soft, rhythmic line derived from the opening theme.

### 3. "Enter Two Girls"

Sleek and sophisticated, the two girls saunter into the bar. The piano music from the previous section provides a large part of the material for this number, whose character is mostly concerned with rhythm (the steady beats in the timpani, the triplet fanfares in the winds) and harmony rather than with creating prominent new themes. The music is distinctly more bluesy than that for the sailors. These are definitely city girls.

### 4. Pas de Deux

As mentioned previously, the music for the outer sections of this number is based on the song "Big Stuff." The tempo is slow, the rhythm hesitant, and the main theme goes to muted trombone followed by muted trumpet. Formally, this piece is a straightforward ABABA. The B section is a perky, staccato interlude in a slightly faster tempo, and you may notice the four-note motto appearing a couple of times in the bass of the piano part. This quicker rhythm generates a wonderful climax and return to the opening theme, a sort of jazzy Tchaikovsky moment that Bernstein must have had a great deal of fun writing. The B music intervenes again for just a couple of bars, before the movement closes in the same mood and tempo in which it began.

### 5. Competition Scene

As you can well imagine, everyone gets involved in this number, and what Bernstein offers is a genuine symphonic development section of all the previous themes and motives. Most prominent, naturally, is the initial music for the three sailors (it undergoes a particularly marvelous transformation as a piano solo later on in the piece), but the ladies' bluesy trombones and triplet fanfares also feature prominently. Because it's a development section, it has to lead to something else, and so this scene rises to a big climax and on a snare drum roll spills over into the . . .

## 6. Three Dance Variations

In the ballet world, a *variation* is merely a solo dance for one of the characters, but of course in music it means something a touch more specific, and Bernstein's three "genre" dances are in fact genuine musical variations. First up is a Galop very similar to those in Shostakovich's ballets of the same period: it's fast, furious, sardonic, and more than a bit hysterical. It follows an ABABA form, with A deriving from the sailor's opening theme, and B featuring the four-note motto on the trumpet and then the trombone.

Like the later, 7/8 Waltz in the *Divertimento*, this example of the genre, following the Galop, never stays in the traditional 3/4 time. The motto appears embedded in the violin melody, but it's easy to hear whenever it glides by. There's a menacing central section very clearly based on the sailor's theme as well—you'll catch it if you notice that its jagged rhythm is basically the same as the one played by the piano in scenes two and three.

Bernstein is always irresistible in Latin mode, and so it proves with this enchanting Mexican Danzón, the last of the three variations. You will surely hear the seeds of *West Side Story* in this piece, but aside from the fact that the main theme (for a pair of flutes) is based on the sailor's tune, this is also the number where the four-note motto features most prominently, initially on the muted trumpet, then in the violins. There are some particularly wonderful touches of orchestration here, including timpani beaten with maracas, just as in the second movement of the "Jeremiah" Symphony. This number comes to a full and decisive close.

## 6. Finale

The finale begins with the women's triplet fanfare, followed immediately by the sailor's theme, and it also recapitulates much of the Scene at the Bar. Expressively, the course of the music is easy to follow: the men get dumped, take a moment to wallow in self-pity (piano solo), then rouse themselves to continue their night of adventure. It's all there in the music, and not the least of Bernstein's accomplishment is that his use of symphonic procedures and variation techniques not only holds the piece together in a formally satisfying way, but by following the various themes and their development over these 25 minutes it becomes possible to understand what must be happening on stage, even if you're only listening to a recording or sitting at a concert. Bernstein's handling of form can't be meaningfully separated from the musical expression, an observation that applies equally to all great music, of whatever period.

## *Facsimile* (1946)

*Scoring: piccolo, 2 flutes, 2 oboes, E-flat clarinet, 2 clarinets, 2 bassoons, 4 horns, cornet, 2 trumpets, 2 trombones, tuba, snare drum, bass drum, cymbals, triangle, woodblock, glockenspiel, timpani, solo piano, and strings*

*Facsimile* is the second of Bernstein's epochal collaborations with dancer and choreographer Jerome Robbins, and in its orchestral guise Bernstein dubbed it a "choreographic essay." The topic is loneliness and the inability of people to forge meaningful relationships. The title suggests the idea of "going through the motions." None of the feelings are genuine: they are only "facsimiles" of the real thing. Conceptually, the ballet has a great deal in common with the Second Symphony ("The Age of Anxiety") based on the Auden poem that appeared the same year that *Facsimile* was completed and performed. It should come as no surprise, then, that Bernstein was immediately taken by a poem that seemed to be operating on the same wavelength as his most recent ballet, and so continued to explore the subject both in the symphony, and later in the opera *Trouble in Tahiti*.

A mere twenty minutes long, *Facsimile* was composed in a burst of concentrated effort lasting Bernstein some three weeks in August 1946, and the work had its theatrical premiere just a couple of months later. Given its subject matter, the music contains fewer popular elements than its predecessor, *Fancy Free*, but it's just as cogently put together. Like the previous ballet as well as "The Age of Anxiety," Bernstein gives a prominent role to the solo piano, not exactly as one of the protagonists, but because pitting a solo voice against the larger ensemble creates a purely musical pattern of interaction among participants that mirrors the happenings on stage particularly well.

The plot is very simple and uncomplicated. A woman is sitting alone and bored on a beach (or some other similarly uninhabited spot), trying to escape her own feelings of desolation. A man enters. The two engage in a flirtation that, despite moments of passion, evaporates as quickly as it began, leaving the two annoyed and unfulfilled. A second man enters, meets the woman, and the two force themselves to try to have a good time. However, it's only when the first man discovers this not very serious "love triangle," and the usual games of jealousy, denunciations, and recriminations ensue, that the three actually believe that they are finally feeling something meaningful. Finally, they realize the pointlessness of it all, the men leave embarrassed, and the woman remains alone as at the start.

Needless to say, this isn't a "happy" story, nor does it contain a number of pictorial or expressive elements that music excels at depicting. It's always problematic for a composer to try to express a futile exercise in shallow emotions and useless activity, and it's risky to try—not because it's hard, but because writing utterly empty, pointless music is so easy. Succeed too well as theater, and the piece itself may well fail to involve the listener on any level at all. On the one hand, the composer needs to give the music an expressive point, but on the other, he needs to put some distance between the emotions—however intense—and his manner of evoking them, letting his audience feel somehow that they aren't quite real. Bernstein achieves this is several ways, and it's this aspect of the music that really commands our attention, far more so than the work's formal or structural elaboration.

## GUIDE TO LISTENING

Although the music of *Facsimile* plays continuously, the work falls into four distinct sections. The first is a portrait of the woman, lonely and bored. Bernstein opens the piece with a classic musical symbol of solitude, a motive for solo oboe. It bears a striking resemblance to the similar evocation of isolation at the opening of the "Scene in the Country" slow movement from Berlioz's *Symphonie fantastique*, another of Bernstein's specialties as a conductor (he recorded it more than once) and a piece that fascinated him throughout his career. Under a gently rhythmic accompaniment in the strings, a more lyrical idea takes shape as a brief duet between flute and piccolo. These two initial themes provide much of the material for the rest of the work. The violins carry the music to a climax, but one that seems singularly tired and listless. A brief flute solo leads the next scene, the Pas de Deux.

This number begins as a waltz, the perfect medium to suggest emotion in terms of stylized, artificial elegance. Like most of Bernstein's waltzes, the rhythm seldom remains in a steady 3/4 meter for very long. At the climax, however, which Bernstein marks "À la Viennoise," the music suddenly turns boisterous and somewhat vulgar, with bass and snare drums emphasizing the "ONE, two, three" rhythm as emphatically and regularly as possible. The waltz dribbles to a quiet close, running out of energy, only to be interrupted by a huge outburst (bass drum roll, cymbal crashes, and tremolo strings), more melodramatic than tragic.

One way to emphasize the artificiality of emotions in music while still expressing them effectively is to exaggerate them, which is precisely the point of this explosion. After a short interjection from the solo piano, the second half of the Pas de Deux begins, turning out to be another exercise in sentimental excess. The strings, *molto vibrato* with "expressive" glissandos, support a duet between two solo violins working in tandem on the one hand, and a solo viola on the other. This, too, remains open ended, returning to the lonely oboe motive that opened the work, here even more doleful on a solo bassoon.

Things perk up with the start of the next scene, the entry of the second man in quicker tempo. This is the longest and most highly developed part of the ballet, music which is for the most part light and charming, with an extensive part for the solo piano. Midway through, as the first man rejoins the flirtatious couple, the mood darkens slightly, but never so much that you get the impression that something truly serious is going on. Despite the potential for negative feelings, the characters continue to have a good time, obviously enjoying the opportunity to raise a bit of a ruckus. This scherzolike scene rises to a powerful climax, then cuts off abruptly.

Without warning, the melodramatic climax from the previous section returns, only now the actual music being recalled is the "lonely" motive from the beginning. The volume and tension slowly drain away, leaving the piano to accompany the flute and piccolo with their wan melodies from the first scene, and the work closes punctually and inevitably with the same oboe solo with which it started. Unlike in the Second Symphony, there is no triumphant apotheosis representing the reaffirmation of faith and hope for the future. *Facsimile* is, in its way, the grittier work, and perhaps the more realistic one as well. Alongside *Fancy Free*, *On the Town*, and "Jeremiah," it confirmed Bernstein's position as a major voice in American music.

## Dybbuk (1974)

*Scoring: tenor and bass-baritone solos, piccolo, 3 flutes, 2 oboes, English horn, E-flat clarinet, 2 clarinets, bass clarinet, 2 bassoons, contrabassoon, 4 horns, 3 trumpets, 3 trombones, tuba, vibraphone, xylophone, glockenspiel, snare drum, tenor drum, 2 bass drums, cymbals, tam-tam, temple blocks, 2 gongs, 2 woodblocks, tom-toms, steel pipe, 2 triangles, castanets, cheesebox, tambourine, low bells, harp, piano, celesta, and strings*

There is a story in many European (and I suspect other) cultures that runs like this: A girl feels abandoned by her fiancé who, unbeknownst to her is actually dead. In her desire to see him again, she utters some sort of foolish oath or blasphemy, and voilà! He turns up and carries her off, promising to marry her. Eventually, she figures out that she's dealing with a ghost and begs him to let her go. Naturally he refuses. Then some kind of struggle ensues, often culminating in a timely prayer to the Virgin Mary or some other appropriate divine power, the sun rises, and the spirit vanishes. At least that's how the story goes in Dvořák's cantata *The Specter's Bride*, the most famous setting of this particular tale. There's also a charming programmatic symphony, "Lenore" (Symphony No. 5) by nineteenth-century composer Joachim Raff, inspired by the same plot, and at least a couple of creaky romantic operas on the subject, too.

The Jewish version of this legend is even creepier. It was turned into a successful play by early twentieth-century Russian/Yiddish author Shlomo Ansky. Two friends, one rich and the other poor, pledge that if they should have a daughter and a son, respectively, then the two children will marry. This duly happens: Leah and Channon arrive, and as they grow up they fall in love. However, Channon's father passes away, and Leah's father conveniently forgets his vow, arranging instead her marriage to a wealthy merchant. In a rage, the religious Channon turns to the Kabbalah, the book of Jewish mysticism, but the power of its magic overwhelms him and he dies, becoming a dybbuk, a disembodied spirit seeking to inhabit a living body. Meanwhile, Leah's wedding is arranged, but at the ceremony Channon enters her and she speaks with his voice. Horrified, the village elders arrange an exorcism to drive out the evil spirit, but not before Leah chooses to join him in oblivion. Channon claims his bride, and Leah's body remains behind, an empty shell.

Hot stuff, isn't it? *Dybbuk* is Bernstein's largest ballet, indeed his longest orchestral work in any form, lasting about fifty minutes. The music fits the plot like a glove, and therein lies the greatest barrier to the work's popularity. At the time of the premiere a lot was made of Bernstein's use of Kabbalistic numerology and other arcane methods of divining twelve-note rows for the music's atonal numbers. Like Wagner, Bernstein enjoyed talking and writing about music as much as actually composing it. He was quite proud of this aspect, too, but perhaps shouldn't have made such a point of it. What matters, after all, is how the music sounds, not the process by which the composer gets there. The actual ballet, Bernstein's first collaboration with Jerome Robbins since their successes of the 1950s, disappointed, which isn't too surprising if you try to imagine a stage full of lithe, limber, dancing Hasidim.

Bernstein, anxious to get the work some exposure in the concert hall, arranged it into two suites, one relatively short and containing only orchestral pieces, the other longer, including the Hebrew chants for tenor and baritone that mingle with some of the more extended numbers. And yet the music does have its admirers (as well it should), most of whom prefer the original version which Bernstein recorded soon after the premiere—and in which form the music was issued on an excellent Naxos disc as well. The two suites were recorded by the composer for Deutsche Grammophon. In the following discussion, I am going to describe the music of the suites because this represents Bernstein's last word on the piece and the music in the complete ballet is the same, just in a different order.

*Dybbuk* is in some ways Bernstein's purest score. There is no jazz, no popular music, and although much of the work is based on Hasidic folk tunes, this aspect has been so thoroughly integrated into the musical fabric that the entire ballet, even the twelve-note bits, sounds all of a piece. In other words, the music contains none of the things that contribute so much to the popularity of Bernstein's other concert works. It is uniformly dark, frightening, and intense. Much of the music is quite spare and hushed. It would make an ideal horror movie soundtrack. The Hebrew prayers (including a setting of the Kaddish) sound as mesmerizing and spooky as anything in *The Omen*. That is not the kind of thing that most people prefer for home (or concert) listening, but film music buffs would probably love it if they knew about it. With familiarity, the music really does get under your skin and become strangely compelling.

## GUIDE TO LISTENING

### Suite No. 1

The first suite, as mentioned, contains all of the vocal music, a series of brief Hebrew chants and prayers arranged as duets for tenor and baritone. The music of these prayers is atonal, which only enhances the weirdness of the experience. As Bernstein himself suggested, the key to writing good atonal music lies in knowing when to use it and what it means, and no one knew better than he. In addition to the sung bits, there are six substantial movements.

### 1. "Invocation and Trance"

After the vocal prelude, the orchestra plays a heavy-footed procession on a theme of markedly Eastern European, Jewish character. This represents the Hasidic community in which the story unfolds. The music approaches and recedes back into silence.

### 2. "The Pledge"

The singers recall the original oath between the two fathers, David and Jonathan, from the First Book of Samuel 20:4: "Whatever your soul desires, I will do it for you." The music is sad and delicate, mostly scored for woodwinds, with gentle support from the strings and harp.

### 3. "Kabbalah"

After an invocation of Leah's name, underpinned by eerie knocking on the tom-toms, the processional "trance" music returns, more colorfully scored. As Channon invokes the demonic spirits, the music increases in speed, spiraling out of control and increasing in power, subsiding only toward the very end.

### 4. "Possession"

This movement follows directly on the previous one, and as you might expect, it's a frenetic dance in broken rhythms that lurches to a violent conclusion.

### 5. Pas de Deux

On Bernstein's recording, this begins with the two singers reciting Kaddish, but in the score the Kaddish comes afterward. Either way, the music represents the dance of Channon (in spirit form) and Leah at the wedding ceremony. It's aptly ghostly, in ABA form, and the central section features a tune for high woodwinds, violin, and celesta that truly sends a shiver down the spine.

### 6. "Exorcism"

In this number, all hell breaks loose with some of the wildest music that Bernstein ever composed. And yet it remains very much in character. Once the dybbuk is expelled from Leah's body, there's a brief return to calm before the ballet ends inconclusively, with the "trance" processional, exactly as it began.

## Suite No. 2

There's a very interesting comparison to be made between this music and the two suites that Sibelius prepared from his incidental music to Shakespeare's *The Tempest*, one for large orchestra, the other for a smaller ensemble. Here the size of the orchestra remains the same as previously, but there are no vocal parts; and as in the Finnish composer's second suite, the music is more subdued, delicate, and overtly melodic. It is, however, no less spooky—not a bit. There are four movements:

### 1. "The Messengers"

As the title suggests, this is a brief whirl of activity suggestion mysterious spirits. The thematic material is elusive, like shapes that stay just out of eyesight, and aside from one sudden climax in the brass, the entire piece maintains a soft dynamic level.

### 2. "Leah"

The most lyrical number in the entire ballet, Leah's music recalls "Miranda" in the Sibelius suite just mentioned, though the tune is Jewish through and through. Cast in a simple ABA form, and led by graceful strings, the music paints a portrait of chaste simplicity and dignity.

### 3. Five Kabbalah Variations

"Leah" leads directly into these variations. Another part of this section from the original ballet found its way into the "Kabbalah" movement of the First Suite, but the five purely orchestral variations have a place here. The eerie knocking on wood from the First Suite reappears, but you don't otherwise need to know the theme at all. This is more "spirit" music, although now the mystical forces convey more power. They scurry and whirl with a cool, malicious brilliance. Some of it may bring to mind the "supernatural" elements in Stravinsky's *The Firebird*.

### 4. "Dream"

A sad string melody leads to the diaphanous middle section where the tick-tock rhythm in the strings under a haunting Jewish melody in the flutes recalls Holst's *The Planets*, or maybe the soundtrack to the film *Alien*. The opening string melody returns—it's one of Bernstein's famously limping waltzes, this case in 5/4 time—and the music evaporates into nothingness.

So the verdict on *Dybbuk*, like that on the "Kaddish" Symphony, is still out. It may always remain a piece for diehard Bernstein fans, but then there are always fine works better suited to the connoisseur than to the casual listener. Give the music a chance, and you'll be rewarded, but there's no need to rush. It's always good to have something special in reserve, awaiting the right moment to be discovered.

## Three Dance Episodes from "On the Town" (1946)

*Scoring: piccolo, flutes, oboe, E-flat clarinet, 3 clarinets, bass clarinet, alto saxophone, 2 horns, 3 trumpets, 3 trombones, tuba, snare drum, bass drum, cymbals, triangle, woodblock, traps, xylophone, timpani, piano, and strings*

The show *On the Town* was unusual for its time, and remains so today, for the amount of dance music that it contains and the importance this has as an integral component of plot development. For this we can thank brilliant dancer-choreographer Jerome Robbins, whose collaborations with Bernstein both on his ballets and on the dance component of his musical comedies created a new standard in American theater. The relationship between the two men, though not without its ups and downs as we might well expect, constitutes one of musical history's great artistic partnerships, once that begs comparison to such famous duos as Strauss/Hoffmansthal, Verdi/Boito, or Mahler/Roller.

*On the Town* itself grew out of the huge success of the ballet *Fancy Free*, which essentially treats the same story: three sailors on shore leave hit New York, looking for girls. In the ballet all of this can be expressed in a succinct twenty-five minutes or so, but a musical comedy requires that the characters have individual identities: the sailors, the girls they meet, and there needs to be a coherent (and hopefully amusing) plot. Of the three sailors, the romantic dreamer is Gaby. Assisted by his colleagues, he embarks on a quest to find, and date, beauty pageant winner Miss Turnstiles, the glamour queen of the New York City subway system.

Two of the three dances included in Bernstein's suite belong to Gaby. The first, a swaggering number that I've seen variously titled "Dance of the Great Lover," just plain "The Great Lover," and my personal favorite, "The Great Lover Exposes Himself," comes from the show's second act. It's a dream sequence in which Gaby, falling asleep on the subway, imagines that he meets Miss Turnstiles and sweeps her off of her feet. The second dance is a pas de deux based on the song "Lonely Town," in which an innocent high school girl meets a sailor in Central Park. She falls for him, but he abandons her. The last dance is an ensemble number, the finale to act 1, which has the entire cast hitting the bars in Time Square, looking for a good time.

As you can see from this description, the order of the dances does not follow that of the musical itself. Bernstein has arranged them so as to make a satisfying sequence for concert performance. It was in fact very unusual to make a serious symphonic work out of dance music from a Broadway show, and Bernstein was well aware of it. In his original program note for the 1946 premiere, he wrote:

> That these are, in their way, symphonic pieces rarely occurs to the audience actually attending the show, so well integrated are all the elements by the master-director George Abbott, the choreographic inventiveness of Jerome Robbins, and the adroitness of the Comden-Green book. Their use, therefore, as concert material is rather in the nature of an experiment.

It was an experiment that scored a major success, and it's interesting to note that even this early in his career Bernstein was referring to the music as "symphonic." What this means in practice is that each number has its own satisfying, internally consistent form. The three dances play for about ten minutes in total, and although short, they do in fact show Bernstein's typical concern for shape and structure, while at the same time admirably fulfilling their role as dance music.

## GUIDE TO LISTENING

### 1. "The Great Lover"

Believe it or not, this jazzy, macho dance number, though it lasts less than two minutes, is written in a perfect "sonata form without development" of exactly the same type that Bernstein uses in the *Candide* Overture or the first movement of his *Serenade*. It even has a clearly defined (if varied) exposition repeat, which is omitted in the recapitulation. You can't imagine how many classical symphonies do exactly the same thing, and always for the same reason: you've heard the themes enough times that there's no need to play them twice when they come around for the last time.

First, there's a brash and bouncing introduction with alternating shots on timpani and suspended cymbals, then the syncopated first theme enters on the violins, always introduced by a six-note trombone "announcement" in descending notes. The second theme follows the first immediately on the woodwind, and it's easier to hear the exact spot where it enters when the exposition gets repeated: just listen for the triangle. At the close of each section, the opening gesture returns as a sort of refrain, and at the end of the dance it introduces a very short coda that brings this brief but certainly symphonically designed movement to a snappy close.

## 2. "Lonely Town": Pas de Deux

This is a slow movement, and again, like many slow movements, it has a simple ABA form. Section A is the actual song "Lonely Town," which creates an atmosphere of gentle nostalgia and introduces the warm violin melody of the central section. The scoring of this opening, with low clarinets and solo trumpet, takes a page straight from the slow movement of George Gershwin's Piano Concerto in F, but the expressive tune in the middle is Bernstein at his romantic best.

## 3. "Times Square: 1944"

One of the many innovations of *On the Town* was its utter currency; operas and musicals like to place their subjects in the past, whether distant or recent, because it gives the authors the necessary distance to allow for creative license. To do otherwise invites ridicule from audiences all too familiar with either the subject or its setting. Verdi found this out the hard way when he chose a contemporary subject for his *La traviata*, and it failed miserably at its premiere (the presence of a chubby young soprano playing the tubercular Violetta didn't help, either). It's easier to pull this off in a comedy, and one thing everyone agreed was that Bernstein's music really sold the concept. Urban, contemporary, smart, and stylish, it *was* New York, 1944.

This is nowhere more true than in the act 1 finale, a ballet that consists of a set of variations on the show's hit tune: "New York, New York (It's a Helluva Town)." There's no need to describe the variations in detail; there's a swanky one for solo saxophone that is particularly sexy. The whole point of this finale is to paint a picture of the colorful variety of popular dance idioms that the characters encounter during their night in Times Square, all unified by the fact that they are based on a single idea representing the actual location itself. It's a splendid concept, and Bernstein pulls it off effortlessly.

Indeed, his arrangement of these three dances creates a miniature but very real symphony: there's an opening movement in traditional sonata form, a slow movement, and a variation finale. This, undoubtedly, is what Bernstein must have meant when he referred to the music as "symphonic." Certainly these *Three Dance Episodes* are fully worthy of that designation, but they also stand as a major example of "the art that conceals art." Their erudition never sounds forced, but rather enhances the delightfully entertaining character of each number.

## Symphonic Suite from "On the Waterfront" (1955)

*Scoring: piccolo, 2 flutes, 2 oboes, E-flat clarinet, 2 clarinets, bass clarinet, alto saxophone, 2 bassoons, contrabassoon, 4 horns, 3 trumpets, 3 trombones, tuba, snare drum, bass drum, cymbals, 2 tam-tams, 3 tuned drums, triangle, woodblock, glockenspiel, vibraphone, xylophone, chimes, timpani (2 players), piano, harp, and strings*

There are major composers, and there are major film composers, and the two seldom meet in one and the same person. Conductor André Previn, himself a composer of no mean accomplishment, once told me that the problem with writing for films is that the circumstances tended to work against "the elongated thought." In other words, you can't write in large forms, and anything you do write might just wind up on the cutting-room floor or be inaudible behind dialogue and other sound effects. The main point of the film, after all, is not to showcase the score.

It has been said that Bernstein was a natural when it came to writing for the silver screen. His technique of constructing larger units from a series of evolving variations on basic thematic material seemed guaranteed to turn out a cohesive yet custom-made piece of work. And yet he only undertook this one project (aside from films of his own musicals, in which he had only limited input). Questions of time and other major commitments aside, the reason undoubtedly stems from Previn's observation about "the elongated thought."

Bernstein did superb work for Elia Kazan's *On the Waterfront*. He was even nominated for an Academy Award (Dmitri Tiomkin actually won that year). But he wasted no time in preparing a "symphonic suite" from his music for the film, and this quickly acquired an independent life that it has enjoyed ever since. Once again, we find Bernstein using that word—*symphonic*—to describe music that, in the normal course of business, should have nothing to do with the concept. As it turns out, he knew perfectly well what he was talking about. *On the Waterfront*, as a study in thematic variation and transformation, is one of the most tightly written pieces that Bernstein ever produced. Had he called it a "symphonic poem" instead of a suite, no one would have batted an eye.

Playing for about twenty minutes in a single movement, the music follows a sort of variation form consisting of an introduction that presents the main theme, followed by four extended variations and a coda. These variations in turn shadow the structure of a traditional symphony: a quick allegro, a slow movement, a dance in moderate tempo, and a fast finale. Of course, the point is not that you need to detect any particular resemblance while listening; what matters is that symphonic form is inherently satisfying in terms of balance of tempos and opportunities for expression, whether here or in works that happen to go by the name *symphony*. As with all of the best symphonies, the actual formal details in this piece arise naturally out of the thematic material itself, and not from the composer trying to squeeze his thoughts into a predetermined shape.

## GUIDE TO LISTENING

The suite opens with a lyrical melody for solo horn, which Bernstein marks to be played "with dignity." There are two points worth noticing about this wonderful tune. First, it has six bars that fall naturally into two equal halves, each half containing three measures in the following meters: 4/4, 4/4, 3/4. The second half of the theme is rhythmically identical to the first, and in fact is a free inversion of it (that is, Bernstein plays the same tune upside down, only not quite exactly). So in a sense, the process of variation is contained within the actual theme itself, but more important, it gives Bernstein plenty of material on which to build the ensuing sections without letting the music become excessively repetitious.

The next thing to notice is that each half of the theme grows from a simple, two-note cell, like a flower petal opening out. Each phrase gains two notes, so first we hear the horn's two-note interval of a rising minor third, then it grows by adding two notes below, then again by adding two notes above. Then the process is reversed for the theme's second half. As important to the subsequent variations as the actual notes of this initial melody is the shape of its phrases. There will be places where you will not hear any specific melodic resemblance, but may notice that the music grows in expanding phrases just like the theme. This is the true art of variation: the ability to work not just with the actual notes of the tune, but with all of its musical parameters.

So the key to following the symphonic course of the music is to know that opening theme. Bernstein gives us plenty of opportunity. It's repeated immediately by the flutes, and then the muted trumpets and woodwinds use the inverted half to bring the introduction to a close. The next section starts immediately, "Presto barbaro." This is music of great violence and excitement—a fight? a chase?—it doesn't matter. The saxophone sneers "crudely" (Bernstein's indication) a motive taken from the theme's inverted half, and with three tuned drums and two timpanists pounding away, Bernstein creates a wild melee of slashing strings and wicked brass sonorities. Like the theme, this section has two well-balanced halves, each of which culminates in the same climax. After the second, the saxophone introduces a brief funeral march on the theme of the Presto (played by the strings "with intensity," embellished by deep strokes on the timpani, tam-tam, and low piano).

The procession approaches and recedes, and then a solo horn reminds us of the main theme. Accompanied by the harp and soft clarinets, a new variant begins gently on the flute. This slow movement has an ABA shape. In the first A section the melody belongs entirely to the flute. The B episode combines the first two notes of the main theme and its inversion simultaneously, while the piano touches in some delicate filigree. Then the A melody returns in the full string section, first violas and cellos, then the violins, then all of the strings plus horns in a climax of tremendous passion. This breaks off suddenly, and a gentle cadence brings back the solo horn, now offstage, once again with the main theme.

The next passage, mostly for strings *fortissimo*, takes up the horn theme and develops it with rich harmony. It is interrupted by another outbreak of fast music, less violent that previously but just as rhythmically charged. Clattering repeated notes on the xylophone, brass, and woodwinds create a diabolical atmosphere. After this brief eruption calm returns by way of preparation for the coda, in which Bernstein builds a huge apotheosis of the main theme accompanied by an ever-increasing crescendo on suspended cymbals and two tam-tams.

It's a very cinematic ending, one that may bring to mind Mussorgsky's *Pictures at an Exhibition* (in Ravel's orchestration), or Mahler's Second Symphony ("Resurrection"). This is actually one of the very few times that Bernstein's music actually comes close to Mahler's, the composer with whom he was most closely associated as a conductor. However, as I hope you will notice, there is nothing about this piece whatsoever that requires you to know anything about the actual events taking place in the film. *On the Waterfront* is as satisfying and complete a piece of "absolute"' music as any symphony of the classical period.

## Symphonic Dances from "West Side Story" (1957)

*Scoring: piccolo, 2 flutes, 2 oboes, English horn, E-flat clarinet, two clarinets, bass clarinet, alto saxophone, 2 bassoons,*

*contrabassoon, 4 horns, 3 trumpets, 3 trombones, tuba,*
*bongos, tambourine, tom-tom, 2 snare drums (one small),*
*conga drum, tenor drum, bass drum, 4 pitched drums, traps,*
*triangle, cymbals, finger cymbals, 3 cowbells, tam-tam,*
*vibraphone, glockenspiel, chime, woodblock, guiro, maracas*
*(large and small), xylophone, police whistle, timpani, harp,*
*piano, celesta, and strings*

*West Side Story* was a landmark in the history of the American theater. In terms of musical sophistication, choreography, and artistic serious- ness (for an ostensible comedy), it was entirely new. Much as been made of the fact that it did not win a Tony Award for Best Musical in the year of its premiere. That honor went to *The Music Man*, also an exceptional piece (let's not be snobby about it), and one far more likely to push all the right buttons among those in charge of passing out prizes. Still, in the half century since its first run, the reputation of *West Side Story* has continued to grow, not just because of the greater respect afforded the masterpieces of American musical theater, but as a result of the endur- ing quality of Bernstein's contribution. The presence of the *Symphonic Dances* on the concert programs of symphony orchestras the world over also has played a noteworthy part in this ongoing reappraisal.

Bernstein had help from colleagues Sid Ramin and Irwin Kostal in the orchestration of the musical, as well as in the arrangement and scoring of this suite for full symphony orchestra. This was only to be expected. Writing for a Broadway pit orchestra is a highly specialized job. For example, in this case, five reed players had to take responsibility for fourteen different woodwind instruments. The string section had no violas. The job of making sure that all the parts got covered, that nothing was out-and-out impossible, that the players had enough time to grab the right instrument both within and between numbers—all of this was a task best left to full-time professional orchestrators, although Sid Ramin stresses that Bernstein discussed "every note in every bar of the score at great length."

The dance element in *West Side Story* plays an unprecedentedly important role in the drama. Bernstein had already shown himself a master composer of ballet in scores such as *Fancy Free* and *Facsimile*, as well as the dance music in his previous musical *On the Town*. This means that *West Side Story* contains a great deal of free-standing orchestral music, just the sort of thing that makes for a perfect concert suite. In this respect, the work isn't much different from, say, Tchaikovsky's *Nutcracker Suite*, or Bizet's Suite from *Carmen*. This particular suite, though, plays continuously. It contains one bit of specially composed music, a flute solo to introduce the conclusion based on the song "I Have a Love," which is also the only bit that is not actual dance music.

More interesting is the designation of this suite as "symphonic." This can mean something as basic as "arranged for symphony orchestra," or it can stand for a more sophisticated handling of the thematic material and the relationships between the individual numbers. Both definitions apply here. From the very first, it was noted that Bernstein's music displayed an unusual degree of unity, of relatedness between its various parts in a way specific to this particular work. He accomplished this harmonically, by basing his most important thematic material on one particularly pungent interval: the tritone (two notes, three whole steps apart). This interval was known as "the Devil in music" during the Middle Ages because of its strange, unsettling dissonance.

If you have a piano or any other musical instrument, you can hear the tritone for yourself simply by playing the notes B and F, either together or one after the other. Play B, then F, then F-sharp, and you have the exotic, haunting motive associated with the name "Maria." The very opening of the suite consists of three notes the last two of which, C and F-sharp, constitute a tritone. This simple motive is so recognizable, and so versatile, that it serves as the perfect device to bind the music of the entire suite together organically. Bernstein was not the first musician to use it this way. One of the composers for whom he had a special affinity, Jean Sibelius, did exactly the same thing in his somber Fourth Symphony, a work that Bernstein knew very well (and recorded).

So the appellation *symphonic* is not only well deserved, it allows Bernstein and his arrangers to organize a suite in which the placement of the individual numbers is designed to create the most effective free-standing musical sequence. There's no need to adopt the same running order as the various numbers appear in a staged performance, nor does the music have to attempt to illustrate any specific action or event. It all hangs together because unity is built into the very fabric of the music, and this undoubtedly contributes in no small degree to the success of the *Symphonic Dances* as an independent concert work. For this reason then, in the discussion that follows we will consider the suite as absolute music, without becoming too concerned with each constituent item's original place in the show.

## GUIDE TO LISTENING

The *Symphonic Dances* plays for about twenty-three minutes, and contains nine short movements.

1. Prologue (CD Track 4)
2. "Somewhere" (CD Track 5)
3. Scherzo (CD Track 6)
4. Mambo (CD Track 7)
5. Cha-cha (CD Track 8)
6. Meeting Scene (CD Track 9)
7. "Cool" Fugue (CD Track 10)
8. "Rumble" (CD Track 11)
9. Finale (CD Track 12)

If you know the musical at all, you can see plainly that the order, Prologue aside, has little or nothing to do with the sequence of events as they unfold on stage. So let's consider each movement individually.

### I. Prologue (CD Track 4)

Performing the same function as an overture, this brief, four-minute Prologue has its own distinct form. Keep in mind the opening gesture: three notes containing the tritone motive, followed by a rapid, three-note "jerk." The Prologue falls into two halves. In the first part, marked "nonchalant," the orchestra (complete with "cool" finger snaps) attempts to assemble a lyrical melody, separated at intervals by the opening gesture. This climaxes with an even bolder return to the opening. Then violence erupts as the tempo increases to a furious allegro (it's actually marked *furioso* at one point), and as you can surely hear this is based mainly on the opening motive, with just enough additional material to provide variety. The presence of Latin percussion suggests the gang conflict that drives the plot forward. The Prologue drives inexorably to a headlong climax interrupted by a blast from the police whistle, and the music rapidly returns to the calm nonchalance in which it began.

## 2. "Somewhere" (CD Track 5)

This is a lovely setting of the musical's most beautiful song, arranged for solo woodwinds and strings. At 6:45 pay particular attention to "I Have a Love," as it appears in the flutes, with a soft accompaniment of harp, piano and gentle tam-tam strokes. Not only does this second song form the perfect coda to "Somewhere," it anticipates its return at the very end of the suite, another example of a "symphonic" procedure used to create unity.

## 3. Scherzo (CD Track 6)

A normal symphonic scherzo usually takes the form AABB, followed by a middle section, or trio, then a recap of the scherzo without repeats (AB). This example is a scherzo in miniature: just the first part, lacking a trio section. It has the form AABBA. The A section ends, tellingly, with the motive "Somewhere," the rhythm of which happens to be the same as the tritone motive that opened the work (the accent is different, on the first note rather than the second). In fact, come to think of it, the entire scherzo consists mostly of melodies built from two-note "Somewhere" fragments. Marvelous, isn't it?

## 4. Mambo (CD Track 7)

This the most famous single number in the entire suite, and certainly one of the greatest single dances ever to hit the Broadway stage. It features a ton of Latin percussion: cowbells, bongos, timbales (tuned drums), and the guiro (scraped gourd), all of which recall the similar Latin percussion in the Prologue. The orchestra even has the option to shout, "Mambo!" at a couple of points. Bernstein has taken great pains to characterize the two gangs musically, and the alternation of these different sound worlds also operates symphonically, as a unifying device. Like most dances, this one has a simple ABA form, the middle section featuring some fabulous licks for the trumpet.

### 5. Cha-cha (CD Track 8)

The delicate Cha-cha, featuring the sounds of finger cymbals and small maracas, is a dance arrangement of the song "Maria," and so it contains within its melody the tritone motive of the opening. It runs directly into the:

### 6. Meeting Scene (CD Track 9)

Also based entirely on "Maria," played by solo strings and vibraphone, this tiny interlude serves as a transition to the "Cool" Fugue.

### 7. "Cool" Fugue (CD Track 10)

This section has two parts. It begins with a setting of the song "Cool," the first two notes of which contain the tritone. At 0:42, the actual fugue begins over a rhythmic accompaniment on the suspended cymbal played with brushes. Its main theme (or "subject") has three phrases separated by pauses. The first two, containing four whole notes apiece, each end with a loud whack on a bongo, so it's easy to hear the fugue's progress. The initial entries of the fugue subject are written for muted trumpet, muted horn and cellos, muted trombone, and then strings. Over all of this, bits of the song "Cool" decorate the fugue subject like so much graffiti on a city building. The fugue culminates in a jazzy, climactic statement of the full song, which then subsides and slinks away to the finger snaps of the Prologue.

### 8. "Rumble" (CD Track 11)

The "Rumble" is a varied recapitulation of the fast music of the Prologue, and so it, too, fulfills a symphonic purpose, bringing the music full circle. It reaches a climax with the most violent repeat of the opening motive thus far, after which (at 1:23), Bernstein's custom-made flute transition leads to the coda.

### 9. Finale (CD Track 12)

The suite concludes as flute and divided strings play "I Have a Love" and "Somewhere," both alternately and in combination, bringing these very symphonic *Symphonic Dances* to a peaceful close.

*West Side Story*, as is well known, is basically a modernized retelling of Shakespeare's *Romeo and Juliet*. Just as the book updated a classic, so Bernstein's music offers a new take on a whole range of musical traditions, reinterpreting both classical (as in serious Western "art" music) and popular (American musical theater) forms and procedures. The piece really is as close as a Broadway show can get to the Wagnerian concept of the "total work of art," in which all of the elements cooperate to create a unified whole, and the *Symphonic Dances* offer the perfect summary of how this totality was achieved on a purely musical level. That it does so in such an entertaining and attractive way, appealing both to hard core classical music enthusiasts as well as pop music fans, is one of those miracles for which the only possible explanation is "genius."

## Three Meditations from "Mass" (1977)

*Scoring: solo cello, harp, timpani, tom-tom, bass drum, cymbals, tambourine, gourds, 3 hand drums, 2 snare drums, triangle, tam-tam, glockenspiel, xylophone, vibraphone, marimba, piano, organ, and strings*

Bernstein's *Mass* remains one of his most controversial pieces: People tend either to love it or hate it (I love it), but even the naysayers agree that it contains splendid music. Most of the issues raised against the work concern it stylistic eclecticism and, of course, matters of taste, though there is so much trendy modern music that goes so much farther in this last respect than Bernstein ever does. It kind of makes you wonder if other factors (jealousy?) are in play. Fortunately this arrangement for cello and orchestra of purely instrumental pieces (and a couple of transcriptions of vocal numbers) avoids most of these questions, and actually works quite well as a sort of mini cello concerto. Of course, if you know all of the original music, hearing it in this arrangement may not be as satisfying, but taken on its own terms the *Three Meditations* offers little cause for complaint.

Like so many twentieth-century works for cello and orchestra, this one was written for Mstislav Rostropovich, whose performances of it (I happened to attend one) were unforgettable. The score suggests a duration for the work of nineteen minutes, but Bernstein and Rostropovich's own recording is closer to seventeen minutes and this actually matters, because a lot of the music is extremely slow and the recording sounds just right: hypnotic but never completely static. Bernstein assembled the complete sequence of three movements over a period of time, arranging the first two mediations for cello and piano, adding the third, then preparing the orchestral versions. And despite the occasional loud outburst make no mistake, these are *meditations*: music of a mostly inward, contemplative quality.

## GUIDE TO LISTENING

### Meditation I: Lento assai, molto sostenuto

During *Mass,* Bernstein wrote, "At certain moments of extreme tension, the Celebrant tries to control the situation by saying 'Let us pray,' and it is that these moments that the *Meditations* are played by the pit orchestra, while the entire company remains motionless in attitudes of prayer, or contemplates ceremonial dance." Well, this isn't quite how it works in the case of the third meditation, but it describes the first two well enough. One point you will notice right away is the scoring for strings and percussion (plus keyboards), a formula Bernstein hit upon initially for the *Serenade,* and which he would use again in *Halil* (for flute and orchestra.) This deployment of forces offers a maximum of opportunities for varied color, with a minimum of balance problems between the soloist and the larger ensemble.

This first Meditation certainly stands among Bernstein's finest and most emotionally gripping slow movements. Its form is very simple: ABABA, although as always the repetitions of each section are varied. The opening section presents an anguished threnody for the cello, accompanied by strings and occasional percussive outbursts from the cymbals and mallet instruments. "With intensity," Bernstein instructs the soloist. After the initial statement of the theme, the organ repeats it, very softly. The actual melody is based on motives that Bernstein also uses in *Mass* for his setting of the "De profundis" text: "From the depths I cried to You, Lord." The music truly does writhe like a soul in torment, the jerky rhythms and extreme tension somehow amplified in being transferred to the solo cello.

The next (B) section provides a complete contrast. Marked "tranquil," it is a lullaby in pure major harmonies, in this context sounding almost heartbreakingly sad. There is a striking melodic similarity between this tune and an important idea in the second movement of Sibelius's Second Symphony. Indeed, although built on a much larger scale, the general emotional tone and form of the Sibelius might well have provided a useful model for this Meditation. It was a symphony that Bernstein knew very well, and conducted often (even doing the finale on one of his televised Young People's Concerts). Regarding the remainder of the movement, which is very easy to follow, merely note that the final return of A, as a brief coda, begins passionately, but subsides quickly into a "mysterious" and "veiled" (Bernstein's terms) calm.

### Meditation No. 2: Andante sostenuto

Bernstein had a lifelong fascination with Beethoven's Ninth Symphony, and with one passage in particular. In the finale, after the infamous double fugue in which the sopranos at the climax shriek their lungs out by holding a high A for what (to them, and in a bad performance to us as well) seems like forever, there's a soft, creepy passage in broken rhythms accompanied by palpitating woodwinds on the text: "You fall prostrate, millions? Do you sense the Creator, O world? Seek him above the starry heavens. Brothers! He must dwell beyond the stars." It's sung by the chorus from the bottom up, starting with the basses (the sopranos are still picking up their vocal cords and putting them back in place), until the full choir reunites on the word "Brothers!"

What makes this passage so remarkable is that it is practically atonal until the cry of "Brothers!" reasserts full, warm, major harmony. Its harmonic instability is what makes it sound so mysterious; and the conflict between tonal and atonal elements in this brief passage represents one of the major defining forces in twentieth-century music generally, and Bernstein's in particular. Order vs. chaos, faith vs. doubt, tonality vs. atonality: however you express it, this theme summarizes the plot of *Mass* perfectly, and it's exactly what this second meditation expresses. Formally speaking, it is a theme plus four variations and a coda. The theme is the creepy sequence from Beethoven's Ninth which, if you know the symphony, you will recognize immediately as it's played pizzicato by the cello in rhythms far more disjointed than anything Beethoven could have imagined.

The first variation has the theme in long notes in the violas, while the cello adds a lyrical melody above. This gains intensity and spills over into the positively terrifying second variation, only three bars long in which the theme is stacked up into a series of grinding, triple forte chords for strings, organ, timpani, and glockenspiel. The third variation, for marimba, cello, organ, strings, and snare drum rolls, is also only three bars long and spreads the theme out again into a single ascending line, decorated by triplet rhythms. Variation four, by contrast, is a hypnotically static series of arpeggios on the piano, interrupted by the beginning of the coda, *fortissimo*, with the consonant harmonies of "Brothers!" (Bernstein actually wrote the German word *Brüder!* under the cello part).

Tonality thus having been reasserted, the rest of the coda returns to the uncertainty of the theme. The cello reprises its lyrical melody from the first variation, then scuttles away to the quick triplet rhythm of the third, getting out of the way just before the movement ends with a startling, percussive bang. This is without doubt some of the most frightening purely instrumental music that Bernstein ever wrote. What makes it all the more fascinating is the fact that he really did stick very closely to Beethoven's original idea, merely following up on some of its more disturbing implications.

## Meditation No. 3: Presto; Molto adagio

This piece assembles music from three different places in *Mass*. It begins with an arrangement for cello of an instrumental solo that Bernstein calls "Epiphany," originally scored for oboe, and later played by a flute. There's a certain naturalness in having this exercise is stylized birdsong played by a woodwind instrument that the cello version cannot match, but again, if you don't have the original in front of you for comparison, this may not matter. What we hear is a free cadenza, underpinned by gently persistent rhythms on a hand drum. These rhythms grow insistently, leading to a wild, exotic dance of vaguely oriental character.

Bernstein's orientalism, however, always sounds like Bernstein, just as Rimsky-Korsakov's or Ravel's sounds equally personal and idiomatic.

Here the cello really comes into its own. Not only is the tune incredibly catchy, Bernstein's frequent use of glissando (sliding) between the notes makes the solo sound like some kind of primitive, Middle Eastern stringed instrument. Plentiful use of "belly dancer" percussion completes the picture. The dance gradually subsides, only to lead to the gentle chorale, "Almighty Father, incline Thine ear." Originally a vocal piece, it both opens and closes *Mass* and its theme is identical to that of the dance, an identity much easier to savor when the two pieces follow one another right away. This arrangement for cello and strings is very slow, hushed, and beautiful. After the first statement of the chorale the "Epiphany" music returns (also the quiet drum taps below), then the chorale once more, before the lonely sounds of the "Epiphany" and the rhythmic drums fade away into silence.

It's worth mentioning that the ending of *Mass* is wholly peaceful and positive, whereas that of the *Three Meditations* is questioning and open ended. This makes sense for a couple of reasons, the first of which stems from the fact that the purely instrumental pieces in *Mass* contain some of its most troubled music, and merely repeating the work's happy ending would have sounded facile and unmotivated. Just as important, we can see that this piece needs to be taken on its own merits as an independent work. As always with Bernstein, it is the music itself that determines its own course, and not some prearranged decision on how it all has to turn out in the end. That this rule holds true even here says something important about how "absolute" a musician Bernstein truly was.

# Chronological List of Works

| Year | Work |
|------|------|
| 1935 | Psalm 148 (voice and keyboard) |
| 1937 | Piano Trio |
| 1938 | Piano Sonata |
| 1940 | Violin Sonata |
| 1942 | Clarinet Sonata; Symphony No. 1 ("Jeremiah") |
| 1943 | *Seven Anniversaries* (piano); *I Hate Music* (song cycle) |
| 1944 | *Fancy Free* (ballet); *On the Town* (musical and *Three Dance Episodes*) |
| 1945 | *Hashkiveinu* (cantor, choir and organ); *Afterthought* (voice and piano) |
| 1946 | *Facsimile* (ballet and *Choreographic Essay*) |
| 1947 | *La Bonne Cuisine* (song cycle); *Simchu Na* (chorus and orchestra/piano); *Reenah* (chorus and orchestra) |
| 1948 | *Brass Music* (four brass and piano); *Four Anniversaries* (piano) |
| 1949 | *Two Love Songs* (voice and piano); Symphony No. 2 ("The Age of Anxiety"); *Prelude, Fugue, and Riffs* (clarinet and jazz ensemble) |
| 1950 | *Peter Pan* (songs and choruses); *Yigdal* (chorus and piano) |
| 1951 | *Five Anniversaries* (piano); *Silhouette* (*Galilee*) (voice and piano) |
| 1952 | *Trouble in Tahiti* (opera) |
| 1953 | *Wonderful Town* (musical) |
| 1954 | *Serenade* after Plato's *Symposium*; *On the Waterfront* (film score and *Symphonic Suite*) |
| 1955 | *The Lark* (French and Latin choruses) |
| 1956 | *Candide* (operetta) |
| 1957 | *West Side Story* (musical, *Symphonic Dances* [1960]) |
| 1958 | *The Firstborn* (incidental music) |
| 1960 | *Bridal Suite* (piano four-hands) |

| Year | Work |
|---|---|
| 1961 | *Two Fanfares* (wind ensemble) |
| 1963 | Symphony No. 3 ("Kaddish") |
| 1965 | *Chichester Psalms* (choir, boy soloist and orchestra) |
| 1968 | "So Pretty" (voice and piano) |
| 1969 | *Shivaree* (double brass ensemble and percussion) |
| 1970 | "Warm-up" (chorus, used in *Mass*) |
| 1971 | *Mass: A Theater Piece for Singers, Players, and Dancers* (*Three Meditations* [1977]) |
| 1973 | "if you can't eat you got to" (male chorus, double bass and piano, adapted in *Songfest*) |
| 1974 | *Dybbuk* (ballet, Suites 1 and 2); "Vayomer Elohim" (voice and piano) |
| 1976 | *1600 Pennsylvania Avenue* (later arranged as *A White House Cantata* [1997]) |
| 1977 | *Songfest*; *Slava!* (overture or band) |
| 1979 | "Up! Up! Up!" and "My New Friends" (voice and piano); *Piccola Serenata* (voice and piano) |
| 1980 | *Divertimento* (orchestra or band); *A Musical Toast* (orchestra or band) |
| 1981 | *Halil*; Touches (piano); "Olympic Hymn" (choir and orchestra) |
| 1982 | *A Quiet Place* (opera) |
| 1986 | "Sean Song" (voice and strings); "Opening Prayer" (baritone and orchestra) |
| 1988 | Missa Brevis (unaccompanied choir with incidental percussion); *Arias and Barcarolles* (piano four-hands, mezzo-soprano, and baritone) |
| 1989 | *Thirteen Anniversaries* (piano); Variations on an Octatonic Scale (recorder and cello); Concerto for Orchestra ("Jubilee Games"); *Dance Suite* (brass quintet) |

# CD Track Listing

All performances feature Leonard Bernstein conducting the New York Philharmonic.

1. Symphony No. 1 ("Jeremiah"): "Prophecy" (7:37)
   From Sony CD 88697 27988 2/2

2. Symphony No. 1 ("Jeremiah"): "Profanation" (6:39)
   From Sony CD 88697 27988 2/2

3. Symphony No. 1 ("Jeremiah"): "Lamentation" (11:28)
   Jennie Tourel, mezzo-soprano
   From Sony CD 88697 27988 2/2

4. *Symphonic Dances from "West Side Story"*: Prologue (4:07)
   From Sony CD 88697 27988 2/1

5. *Symphonic Dances from "West Side Story"*: "Somewhere" (3:52)
   From Sony CD 88697 27988 2/1

6. *Symphonic Dances from "West Side Story"*: Scherzo (1:18)
   From Sony CD 88697 27988 2/1

7. *Symphonic Dances from "West Side Story"*: Mambo (2:15)
   From Sony CD 88697 27988 2/1

8. *Symphonic Dances from "West Side Story"*: Cha-cha (0:54)
   From Sony CD 88697 27988 2/1

9. *Symphonic Dances from "West Side Story"*: Meeting Scene (0:47)
   From Sony CD 88697 27988 2/1

10. *Symphonic Dances from "West Side Story"*: "Cool" Fugue (3:03)
    From Sony CD 88697 27988 2/1

11. *Symphonic Dances from "West Side Story"*: "Rumble" (1:52)
    From Sony CD 88697 27988 2/1

12. *Symphonic Dances from "West Side Story"*: Finale (2:50)
    From Sony CD 88697 27988 2/1

13. *Serenade* after Plato's *Symposium*: "Phaedrus: Pausanias"
    (Lento: Allegro) (7:03)
    Zino Francescatti, violin
    From Sony CD 88697 27988 2/5

14. *Serenade* after Plato's *Symposium*: "Aristophanes" (Allegretto)
    (4:08)
    Zino Francescatti, violin
    From Sony CD 88697 27988 2/5

15. *Serenade* after Plato's *Symposium*: "Erixymachos" (Presto) (1:28)
    Zino Francescatti, violin
    From Sony CD 88697 27988 2/5

16. *Serenade* after Plato's *Symposium*: "Agathon" (Adagio) (6:53)
    Zino Francescatti, violin
    From Sony CD 88697 27988 2/5

17. *Serenade* after Plato's *Symposium*: "Socrates: Alcibiades"
    (Molto tenuto: Allegro molto vivace) (10:55)
    Zino Francescatti, violin
    From Sony CD 88697 27988 2/5

Under license from SONY Custom Marketing Group,
SONY MUSIC ENTERTAINMENT

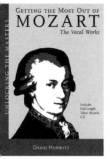

GETTING THE MOST OUT OF
**MOZART**
The Vocal Works

Includes
Full-Length
Tracks Records
CD

UNLOCKING THE MASTERS

DAVID HURWITZ

# UNLOCKING THE MASTERS

The highly acclaimed Unlocking the Masters series brings readers into the world of the greatest composers and their music. All books come with CDs that have tracks taken from the world's foremost libraries of recorded classics, bringing the music to life.

"With infectious enthusiasm and keen insight, the Unlocking the Masters series succeeds in opening our eyes, ears, hearts, and minds to the great composers." – *Strings*

---

**BACH'S CHORAL MUSIC:
A LISTENER'S GUIDE**
by Gordon Jones
$22.99 • 978-1-57467-180-3
HL00332767

**BACH'S KEYBOARD MUSIC:
A LISTENER'S GUIDE**
by Victor Lederer
$22.99 • 978-1-57467-182-7
HL00332830

**BEETHOVEN'S PIANO MUSIC:
A LISTENER'S GUIDE**
by Victor Lederer
$22.99 • 978-1-57467-194-0
HL00333060

**BEETHOVEN'S SYMPHONIES:
A GUIDED TOUR**
by John Bell Young
$22.99 • 978-1-57467-169-8
HL00331951

**BERNSTEIN'S ORCHESTRAL MUSIC:
AN OWNER'S MANUAL**
by David Hurwitz
$24.99 • 978-1-57467-193-3
HL00332912

**BRAHMS: A LISTENER'S GUIDE**
by John Bell Young
$22.99 • 978-1-57467-171-1
HL00331974

**CHOPIN: A LISTENER'S GUIDE
TO THE MASTER OF THE PIANO**
by Victor Lederer
$22.95 • 978-1-57467-148-3
HL00331699

**DEBUSSY:
THE QUIET REVOLUTIONARY**
by Victor Lederer
$22.95 • 978-1-57467-153-7
HL00331743

**DVOŘÁK: ROMANTIC MUSIC'S
MOST VERSATILE GENIUS**
by David Hurwitz
$27.95 • 978-1-57467-107-0
HL00331662

**THE GREAT INSTRUMENTAL WORKS**
by M. Owen Lee
$27.95 • 978-1-57467-117-9
HL00331672

**EXPLORING HAYDN:
A LISTENER'S GUIDE TO
MUSIC'S BOLDEST INNOVATOR**
by David Hurwitz
$27.95 • 978-1-57467-116-2
HL00331671

**LISZT: A LISTENER'S GUIDE**
by John Bell Young
$22.99 • 978-1-57467-170-4
HL00331952

**THE MAHLER SYMPHONIES:
AN OWNER'S MANUAL**
by David Hurwitz
$22.99 • 978-1-57467-099-8
HL00331650

**OPERA'S FIRST MASTER:
THE MUSICAL DRAMAS OF
CLAUDIO MONTEVERDI**
by Mark Ringer
$29.95 • 978-1-57467-110-0
HL00331665

**GETTING THE MOST OUT OF
MOZART:
THE INSTRUMENTAL WORKS**
by David Hurwitz
$22.95 • 978-1-57467-096-7
HL00331648

**GETTING THE MOST OUT OF
MOZART: THE VOCAL WORKS**
by David Hurwitz
$22.95 • 978-1-57467-106-3
HL00331661

**PUCCINI:
A LISTENER'S GUIDE**
by John Bell Young
$22.95 • 978-1-57467-172-8
HL00331975

**SCHUBERT: A SURVEY OF HIS
SYMPHONIC, PIANO, AND
CHAMBER MUSIC**
by John Bell Young
$22.99 • 978-1-57467-177-3
HL00332766

**SCHUBERT'S THEATER OF SONG:
A LISTENER'S GUIDE**
by Mark Ringer
$22.99 • 978-1-57467-176-6
HL00331973

**SHOSTAKOVICH SYMPHONIES
AND CONCERTOS:
AN OWNER'S MANUAL**
by David Hurwitz
$22.99 • 978-1-57467-131-5
HL00331692

**SIBELIUS, THE ORCHESTRAL
WORKS: AN OWNER'S MANUAL**
by David Hurwitz
$27.95 • 978-1-57467-149-0
HL00331735

**TCHAIKOVSKY:
A LISTENER'S GUIDE**
by Daniel Felsenfeld
$27.95 • 978-1-57467-134-6
HL00331697

**DECODING WAGNER:
AN INVITATION TO HIS WORLD
OF MUSIC DRAMA**
by Thomas May
$27.99 • 978-1-57467-097-4
HL00331649

**AMADEUS
PRESS**
www.amadeuspress.com

Prices and availability subject to change
without notice.